Drupal 6 Content Administration

Maintain, add, and edit the content of your Drupal site
with ease

J. Ayen Green

PUBLISHING

BIRMINGHAM - MUMBAI

Drupal 6 Content Administration

Copyright © 2009 Packt Publishing

First published: June 2009

Production Reference: 1190609

Published by Packt Publishing Ltd.
32 Lincoln Road
Olton
Birmingham, B27 6PA, UK.

ISBN 978-1-847198-56-3

www.packtpub.com

Cover Image by Parag Kadam (paragvkadam@gmail.com)

Credits

Author
J. Ayen Green

Reviewers
Edward Peters
John K. Murphy

Acquisition Editor
David Barnes

Development Editor
Dilip Venkatesh

Technical Editor
Hithesh Uchil

Copy Editor
Leonard D'Silva

Indexer
Monica Ajmera

Editorial Team Leader
Akshara Aware

Project Team Leader
Priya Mukherji

Project Coordinator
Zainab Bagasrawala

Proofreader
Dirk Manuel

Production Coordinator
Shantanu Zagade

Cover Work
Shantanu Zagade

About the Author

J. Ayen Green is a software and web site developer, writer, and poet. He is the chief software architect at Ayen Designs. He and his wife, Sofía-Aileen, make their home in New York City.

Some might look at writing a technical book as paint-by-numbers as compared to the oil painting of a novel. With no intention of minimizing the talent needed for the latter, I have to argue that keeping a reader's interest is far easier when writing about a serial killer appearing in a doorway, than it is while writing about HTML tags. That said, it's been an enjoyable experience, and I'd like to take the time to thank the people responsible for that.

My wife, Sofia-Aileen, handled her near-widow status over the past several months with an aplomb that created a stress-free work environment for me. I hope she didn't get too used to being 'single'.

The experience of working with Frank Bozak, the owner of the web site `MusicToHealBy.com`, the example in this book, was what one dares to hope for from a composer of music for the soul. He's been patient, enthusiastic, and receptive, eagerly anticipating the climax. It takes much longer to finish when you have to stop and write about each step along the way.

The staff at Packt are a delight to work with. In addition to the nameless army out there who make things happen, my thanks go out to David Barnes, Dilip Venkatesh, Zainab Bagasrawala, Abhijeet Deobhakta, and Hithesh Uchil for their dedication to producing the best product while keeping the writer alive, as well as to John K. Murphy and Edward Peters for a great job as technical reviewers.

Finally, I must not fail to mention the enormously talented designers, coders, and technical writers who continue to make Drupal one of the best software titles ever released.

About the Reviewers

Edward Peters has worked for all of his adult life with Initiatives of Change (IofC), an international trust-building network (www.iofc.org). Between 2002 and 2008 he managed IofC's global Internet operation, servicing the needs of activists in many countries and many languages. In 2008, he oversaw the move of the organization's proprietary Web CMS into the Drupal framework—a technically-challenging task, given the objective of achieving a multi-lingual, multi-site system running off one codebase and one database, with user and content sharing across all sites.

Edward also does freelance web development work for a number of small clients (www.edwardpeters.co.uk) and is moving several of them into the Drupal framework. He attended DrupalCons in Boston and Washington D.C., and is enthusiastic about Drupal and the Drupal community.

He served as a technical reviewer for another Packt publication, *Learning Drupal 6*, by Matt Butcher.

John K. Murphy is a graduate of the University of West Virginia and has been wrapped up in computers and software development since the 1980's. When he is not buried in a book or jumping out of an airplane, he works as an IT consultant.

John lives with his wife and two children in Pittsburgh, PA and is currently obsessing about the Internet of Things.

This book is dedicated to Scott Corley, one of those people who can see the forest for the trees. He's rescued me more than once, but most notably the first time, in college, when, with his gentle and diplomatic flair, he remarked, "Hey [expletive deleted], have you noticed that you're busting your butt in chemistry, and meanwhile you're acing the computer stuff without studying?"

Thanks, Fonzo.

Table of Contents

Preface

This book is a quick-start guide that best serves Drupal Content Editors. The author's experience enables him to explain, in an efficient and interactive manner, how you can keep your site up-to-date. This book begins with a discussion of content management and Drupal, and then teaches you how to create content, add elements to it, and make the content findable. You will then learn to set up the framework for a creative team and the various options for editing content offline, their benefits and pitfalls. This book helps you to quickly and easily solve problems, and manage content and users for a web site. It will help users to become more effective and efficient managers of Drupal-based web sites.

What this book covers

In every chapter you will find discussions and activities on an aspect of Drupal meaningful to the Content Editor. Each chapter builds on the knowledge gained from the prior chapters. Following is a summary of each chapter:

Chapter 1-The Grand Tour

The beginning of the journey:

- About Drupal
- About a Content Management System
- The target audience
- What will be done in the chapters
- A tour of Drupal

Chapter 2 – Content Creation

Creating page and story content from the user side:

- The methods of entering text (plain text, plain text with tags, Rich Text Editor)
- The other fields that can be present on the content submission screen
- The various content creation and editing capabilities that can be allowed or denied for each type of user
- Create a new article using plain text by pasting and then adding to it
- Create an article with additional formatting, by using tags
- Create a story using a Rich Text Editor

Chapter 3 – Content Seasoning

Adding elements to your content to spice it up:

- Teasers
- Links
- Images
- Embedded sound
- Embedded video
- PDFs
- Attachments and uploading

Create an article to promote a new CD, with:

- A teaser for the front page
- A link to the artist's web site
- An image of the CD cover
- A clip of the music
- A video of the artist commenting on his work

Chapter 4 – Content Editing

The elements of basic content administration:

- Full HTML and PHP content input
- Revisions
- Making some changes to the article that you have created
- Using a PHP snippet to provide content
- Editing a revised article

Chapter 5 – Making Content Findable

What to do with the content so readers can find it:

- Paths, taxonomy and tags
- Publishing the article created in the previous chapter
- Performing some basic Search Engine Optimization by creating a URL and category tags to complement the content

Chapter 6 – Rich Content Types

Understanding the most popular Rich Content types available and their uses:

- Blogs
- Blocks
- Views
- Creating a text block in order to make content available in multiple locations
- Creating a video block to use in the site margin
- Creating a view to display content of similar subject matter
- Creating a blog entry

Chapter 7 – Building a Team

When a site moves from static content or low-volume content to something larger, more people are needed, as are more specific operational roles. You will learn about the tools available for enabling this:

- Roles
- Content types
- Permissions
- Access Rules
- Post Settings

Setting up the framework for a creative team:

- Create a new role so that you can have editors
- Allow for a hierarchy of Content Editors — Block Editors, Article Editors, and overall Content Editors

Chapter 8 – Offline Content Creation

Options for editing content offline, their benefits, and pitfalls:

- Cutting and pasting
- Blog API
- Mailhandler
- Using each of the methods that you have learned to send content to the project site

Appendix A

- Downloading and installing a 'clean' copy of Drupal
- Downloading Drupal
- Creating a MySQL database
- Installing Drupal
- Confirming that it works

Appendix B

Where to find:

- Help
- Documentation
- Modules
- Themes
- More Packt guides

Who this book is for

This book is designed for those who run the site day-to-day but didn't set it up, and aren't necessarily that well versed in Drupal or web technologies.

You could be a Content Editor, Proofreader, Graphic Artist, Feature Editor, or anyone else concerned with managing content on a Drupal installation.

Conventions

In this book, you will find a number of styles of text that distinguish between different kinds of information. Here are some examples of these styles, and an explanation of their meaning.

Code words in text are shown as follows: "The `date()` command generates a date in the format."

A block of code will be set as follows:

```
#ref-footer span {
    font-family: Tahoma, Arial, sans-serif;
    font-size: 10pt;
    font-weight: bold
    position: relative;
    top: 30%;
    margin-top: -24px
}
```

New terms and **important words** are shown in bold. Words that you see on the screen, in menus or dialog boxes for example, appear in our text like this: "In the **Create Div Container** pop-up, we'll click on the **Advanced** tag".

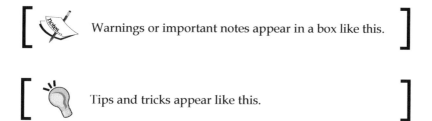

Warnings or important notes appear in a box like this.

Tips and tricks appear like this.

Reader feedback

Feedback from our readers is always welcome. Let us know what you think about this book—what you liked or may have disliked. Reader feedback is important for us to develop titles that you really get the most out of.

To send us general feedback, simply send an email to `feedback@packtpub.com`, and mention the book title in the subject of your message.

If there is a book that you need and would like to see us publish, please send us a note via the **SUGGEST A TITLE** form on `www.packtpub.com`, or send an email to `suggest@packtpub.com`.

If there is a topic that you have expertise in and you are interested in either writing or contributing to a book, then see our author guide on www.packtpub.com/authors.

Customer support

Now that you are the proud owner of a Packt book, we have a number of things to help you to get the most from your purchase.

Errata

Although we have taken every care to ensure the accuracy of our contents, mistakes do happen. If you find a mistake in one of our books—maybe a mistake in the text or in the code—we would be grateful if you would report this to us. When you do so, you can save other readers from frustration, and help us to improve subsequent versions of this book. If you find any errata, please report them by visiting http://www.packtpub.com/support, selecting your book, clicking on the **let us know** link, and entering the details of your errata. Once your errata are verified, your submission will be accepted and the errata added to any list of existing errata. Any existing errata can be viewed by selecting your title from http://www.packtpub.com/support.

Piracy

Piracy of copyright material on the Internet is an ongoing problem across all media. At Packt, we take the protection of our copyright and licenses very seriously. If you come across any illegal copies of our works in any form on the Internet, please provide us with the location address or web site name immediately so that we can pursue a remedy.

Please contact us at copyright@packtpub.com with a link to the suspected pirated material.

We appreciate your help in protecting our authors, and our ability to bring you valuable content.

Questions

You can contact us at questions@packtpub.com if you are having a problem with any aspect of the book, and we will do our best to address it.

1
The Grand Tour

Every book is a journey, and here we are at the beginning. You may be standing in the bookstore, having just opened this book to the first chapter, wondering whether this is the right book for you, or whether you should be reaching for the 1,200 page 'encyclopedia' next to it. This is the sole information-only chapter in this book. All of the other chapters have hands-on activities to help you get up to speed quickly.

You might be wondering what 'Drupal' is! So, let's start out by telling you where we're going, why we're going there, and whether it's in your interest to come along.

What will I learn?

In this chapter, we will outline:

- What Drupal is
- What a Content Management System is
- Who the intended reader is
- What you will be doing in the chapters
- A high-level description of how Drupal is organized

What is Drupal?

> *"Drupal is a free software package that allows an individual or a community of users to easily publish, manage, and organize a wide variety of content on a web site."*

That is an excerpt from the Drupal web site. To paraphrase it, Drupal is a **CMS (Content Management System)** engine. It is used to create and administer CMS web sites.

What is a Content Management System?

The traditional model for a web site has been a file for each page. The 'home page' might be a file named index.html, and for the About Us page, another file named about.html. This model works fine for an unchanging (static) 'Hello—here is what we do—come see us—Bye' site, but for a site where the content changes often, or a site where showcasing content is what you do, it's a horrible model for someone who is not a web site developer to maintain.

With a CMS, the goal is to segregate the content (the text and images) from all of the cryptic computerese, so that in many cases, adding and editing content is no more complicated than creating a document in your favorite text editor.

Who is the target reader?

There are basically five types of computer books that can be bought on a given topic:

- **Pocket guide**—contains the bare essentials of the topic (like a 'cheat-sheet'). The audience is a reader who is very familiar with the topic.

- **Reference manual**—contains a summary of the most-used features. The audience is a reader who is already knowledgeable about the topic.

- **Learning guide** (User's Guide, Developer's Guide, Administrator's Guide)—contains a narrative approach for learning the topic, in its entirety, from start to finish. The audience is a reader who is new to the topic.

- **Encyclopedia**—contains every aspect of the topic. The audience is typically a software developer, graphics designer, or someone who needs to use the subject technology at the expert-level.

- **Quick-start guide**—contains a targeted subset of the topic. The audience is a novice wanting to jump-in with their sleeves rolled up.

This book is a quick-start guide. In the world of Content Management Systems, the administrators run the site and keep it on-line, the Content Editors create, edit, and publish content, and the Users view the content. This book best-serves the Content Editor. It's not an exhaustive blow-by-blow account of every aspect of Drupal like an 'encyclopedia' would be, but instead, it's a small selection of information and activities aimed at imparting knowledge in an efficient and interactive manner.

What will I do in the chapters?

The chapters in this book have some activities incorporated into them, where in we will:

- Take text and create Drupal content from it
- Edit and format the content using HTML, CSS, and a Rich Text Editor
- Add teasers, links, images, sounds, and videos in order to spice things up
- Add downloadable content
- Create revisions
- Use a PHP snippet
- Define custom URLs and tags in order to be ranked more favorably by the search engines
- Create a blog entry, both online and offline
- Create an ad block
- Create content via email
- Create custom content presentations—Views
- Define the roles necessary for a creative team and their capabilities

A guided tour of Drupal

In a way, Drupal is like a house. The look and arrangement may vary, but there will always be certain types of rooms that every house has (such as a kitchen, a bedroom, and a place where the 'administrative' things take place, such as the hot water heater, water shut-off valve, and so on). With Drupal, you begin with a framework. It comes with some standard themes that affect the way it looks. Custom themes can be created or obtained to alter the look even more. Having said that, there will always be two parts to a Drupal site:

- The front end—this is the part of the web site that a site visitor sees, where the content is presented
- The back end (or Admin panel)—this is part that the site staff see, where the workings of the site are controlled, and the appearance of the site is adjusted

There are various parts to the front end, many of which depend on the arrangement of the content, and many parts to the back end in the way of administrative pages. Because of the condensed format of this book, we're going to jump around quite a bit, so let's take a little time now to look at a site. Think of this as the 'getting started' guide that you get on a folded piece of paper with your new computer or stereo component, and that includes an illustration and a description of the component's buttons and switches.

The Drupal front end

First, let's take a look at what the home page (the front page in Drupal parlance) of a Drupal web site looks like. We'll look at two: an "out of the box no changes have been made" front page, and a front page for the site that we'll be using throughout the book, http://musictohealby.com.

The following screenshot shows the Drupal front page of a newly-created site. There are a few areas on the web page to note, and these have been highlighted with large numbers:

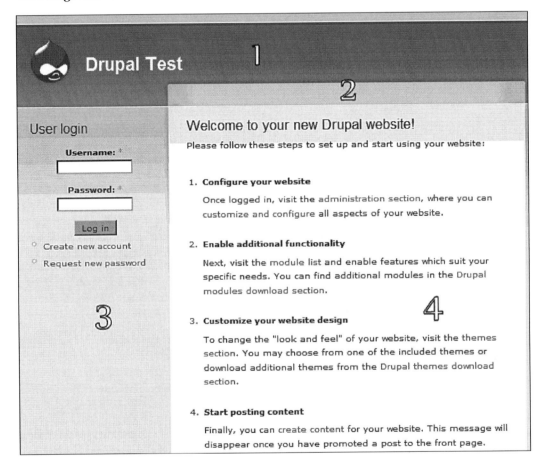

A brief description of the areas on the web page that we have highlighted is as follows:

1. The **header** area—here you will find the site name, logo, and the banner. Some sites also have a few links in this section, or a few words excerpted from content as a link to the content.

2. The **top navigation** area—this is typically where the main links to other pages on the site will be.

3. The **left navigation** area—although some pages may have a right-hand navigation area (or both right-hand and left-hand, or none) this is usually where the user login panel, if used, will be, as well as additional links to site locations.

4. The **content** area—content appears in predetermined sections of the page, called regions. There is almost always a main content region. There can be additional content areas, and other regions for what are known as **Blocks**, which are used for ads, small amounts of content, and other things.

It may not look like much, but the part that you don't see is the powerful 'engine' under the Drupal hood that allows a developer to turn this into a rich site. The following screenshot shows the same engine with a custom theme applied to it and some content added.

Areas 1 to 4, in the screenshot that we have just seen, represent the same areas as they did in the screenshot preceding it. However, you can see that in (2) there are two sets of links in the top navigation area, (3) has links in the left-hand navigation area, (4) has several content areas, and (5) has blocks in the right-hand navigation area.

The Drupal back end

The back end of the Drupal framework is known as the admin panel, and it's here where most of the business takes place. The following screenshot shows the main administrative menu of the site that we'll be using. It has some sections that are supplemental to what the menu would have after a new installation.

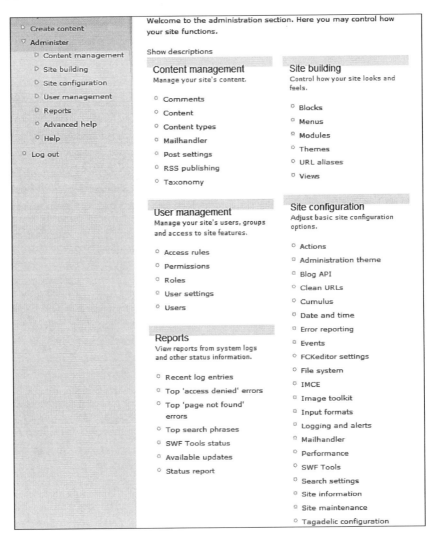

The following is a short description of the use of each area. You can treat this section as a reference. The main understanding to take from it is that almost all of the functions that you will need to perform as a Copy Editor are done through the administrative panel.

Create content

This section appears in the left-most navigation area, but not in the main admin area. This is because, technically, it's not an administrative function. This is where articles and the like are created.

Content management

The Content management area is where the Content Editor is going to spend most of his or her time. Eventually, you will learn the URL shortcuts to these areas. For example, the Content section, where nodes are edited, is reachable via `/admin/content/node`.

Comments

Drupal gives you the ability to allow site visitors to comment on content. You can control whether the visitor has to be registered to do this, and whether comments will be published upon being created, or whether they must be approved of.

Content

This is the area where existing content can be edited, 'published' for others to see, revised, and 'promoted'. It makes a piece of content available to appear on the front page. This is probably where 99% of your time will be spent.

Content types

There are two types of content available initially, a Page and a Story (article). New types can be created. For example, the calendar in the **Music To Heal By** front page uses a content type of Event.

Mailhandler

Drupal can have functionality added to it as (free) options, known as modules. This module allows content to be created via email. There will be an activity regarding this capability in Chapter 8.

Post settings

Some CMS sites are created to allow visitors to register and create their own content, for example, a social site for writers. This section allows you to set standards for 'posts', which are contributed content.

RSS publishing

People can subscribe to your site and be notified when new content is published. Think of it as a free, on-demand direct mail campaign!

Taxonomy

You may have run into 'tags' on other sites. These are categorical terms used to group items together, and to make it easier to search. This section allows the creation of 'vocabularies' that will contain such terms.

User management

Before you start adding users, you'll want to configure the way in which users are added. User management allows you to create a user account, and administer the privileges for the user, on your Drupal web site.

Access rules

From here you can control which users and domains can access your site.

Permissions

Most actions performed in Drupal have an associated 'permission' that grants a type of user an ability. Permissions will allow you to differentiate the capabilities of one type of user from another.

Roles

Roles are the types of users, such as editor, administrator, and so on. They are created and managed here, and the functions that they are allowed to access are defined via permissions.

User settings

Here, you can define whether users can register for the site, and if so, whether they receive a welcoming email.

Users

Here is where user ID's are created and are assigned to a user role.

Reports

We won't go through every option listed in this section, but here is where you can view dynamic reports that will be useful for administering the site, including the all-important **Status report**, which reveals the 'health' of the site.

Site building

This section controls how your site looks and feels.

Blocks

Blocks are small pieces of content, such as advertisements. They are created here, and assigned to regions on the page.

Menus

Menus are the navigation links on the page. You can create as many menus as you need.

Modules

Modules are the code that makes the site work, and the add-ons that give the site more functionality. They are controlled from here.

Themes

A theme is a visual design for the site, and what makes the basic Drupal installation site different from the **Music To Heal By** site. They are configured here, and then enabled.

URL aliases

URL aliases allow you to specify what the URL of a given page will be, rather than using the Drupal defaults, which are not very user-friendly.

Views

The front page will show more than one piece of content at a time, if there is more than one content area defined. However, having a page that shows multiple pieces of content, based on a common category or topic, is often required. A View allows this. They are created and maintained here. Views are not a part of the core Drupal installation. They are provided by an add-on module. However, for any site with templated content, or pages with a multifaceted layout, Views are a must-have.

Site configuration

The Site configuration options are used for the Drupal site's configuration, and are meant for the site administrator. File system settings, error logs, site settings, and even shutting the site down for maintenance are done from here.

Summary

As you can see, Drupal provides a rich environment for publishing content for your visitors or members. Publishing content for a new Drupal installation can be accomplished in very little time.

In the chapters that follow, you will find carefully-selected discussions and activities, which are aimed not at making you a Drupal expert, but at giving you much breadth and a little depth in understanding what capabilities are available to you, just like someone giving you a tour of the town to which you're considering moving.

In Chapter 2, we'll start some hands-on activities, where you will learn about creating content for your Drupal site.

2
Content Creation

By its very nature, Drupal is a **Content Management System (CMS)**. Unlike web sites that are built around image libraries or shopping carts, a CMS is driven by content, usually in the form of text, images, videos, and the like. Creating, editing, and "filing" content is as fundamental an operation in Drupal as is doing the same with your financial transactions in Quickbooks.

Simply having a large amount of text in a giant repository would make the task of finding and using what you need excruciating. A good CMS makes it easy for you to add, organize, and use content. Think of a magazine. Some pages are entirely composed of one story. Some have two or more articles of related content, and some, two or more articles of unrelated content. In order to compose a page comprised of small articles about leafy green vegetables, you have to be able to create and find them. Drupal provides the creation and arrangement of pieces, and this is what you will learn next.

What you will learn

In this chapter, you will learn about:

- The types of content that exist in Drupal
- The process of creating Page and Story content
- The methods of entering content (plain text, plain text with tags, Rich Text Editor)
- The fields that are used in content submission
- Assigning content creation and editing capabilities to the site's users

What you will do

In this chapter, you will:

- Create a new page using plain text by pasting
- Add additional text to your page
- Format your page, using HTML tags
- Create a story using a rich text editor

Understanding content in Drupal

In order to get the most out of Drupal with the least confusion, a basic understanding of some concepts is needed; the most important of these is 'content', because we're working with a Content Management System.

What is content?

We can surely answer a simple question such as "Is a paragraph of text, *content*?" However, while we might consider a paragraph of text to be content, with Drupal, the answer to that question is: "It depends".

Opinions on how best to express what is, and is not, content in Drupal vary greatly. It helps if we differentiate 'content' from **Drupal content**. We can certainly say that 'content' is any material that makes up the web page, be it Drupal-generated content, such as the banner and buttons, or user content, such as the text of a blog. Within Drupal, 'content' has more narrow parameters.

When you create a story in Drupal, it is stored in a database as a **node**, and is assigned a **node ID (nid)**. Some would say that, with respect to Drupal, content is limited to objects (stories, and so on) that can receive comments created by users, and are assigned a node id. Others say that it is any object in Drupal that can be on a page. These technical discussions can cause your eyes to glaze over. It would seem that the latter definition makes the most sense; however, there is one additional factor that we need to consider, and that is the layout of the Drupal admin functions.

Drupal provides admin functions for creating and maintaining content, and these functions list only those objects that receive a node id. Other objects, such as **Blocks**, which we'll cover in Chapter 6, are created and maintained elsewhere.

So, in order to avoid confusion, let's agree on the following terminology:

- **Content**—will be any content on a page
- **Node Content**—will be limited to pages, stories, and any other types administered under the Content Management umbrella within Drupal
- **Rich Content**—will be referred to by its specific type, such as Blocks and Views

Node Content types—the Story

Drupal comes with two predefined Node Content types: **Story** and **Page**. Let's begin by working with a Story.

 Although Drupal only provides two Node Content types, it is easy to define new ones, such as News and Blog. A reason for doing this is that different types of site users can be given the ability to create certain Node Content types but not others.

Drupal defines a Story as being:

"ideal for creating and displaying content that informs or engages web site [sic] visitor"

The definition mentioned above isn't really a precise definition. This is because if we accept it, then we can infer that the other Node Content type must be the one that bores the life out of visitors!

With its default settings, a Story is designed to be the type of page content that the visitor has come to the site to read. If not overridden, this will become part of the pool of Node Content from which the front page (home page) is composed. Additionally, visitors to the site will be allowed to post comments about the Story. Personally I feel that 'Article' or 'Piece' would have been a more descriptive name than 'Story'. Drupal allows you to name the Node Content types—even the predefined ones—anything you want. Therefore, if you feel strongly about the name of a Node Content type, then change it!

 The 'home page' of a Drupal site is called the 'front page', in keeping with a newspaper. Unlike a typical web site, where this page content remains relatively unchanged, the default for a Drupal site is that the front page self-composes from available Stories, as well as any Node Content that has been 'promoted'.

This is a good time for an activity, and as luck would have it, our project site needs a new Story. Let's create one.

Activity 2.1: Creating a Story

We're going to create a Story to use on our project site's front page. The Story will be used to promote a new CD. You can feel free to alter the subject to anything you feel comfortable with, by knocking out a couple of paragraphs.

Although you can use Drupal to compose your Story or any other Node Content, which is something that we'll do in another activity, many people prefer to compose 'offline' in their favorite text editor, and then later copy and paste that content into Drupal. We'll use that method in this example.

1. Open your favorite text editor and type a few lines to promote a new CD. If you're not feeling creative, then feel free to just copy the text used below. I'll use **WordPad** (shown here in the screenshot) as the editor, but any text editor will do.

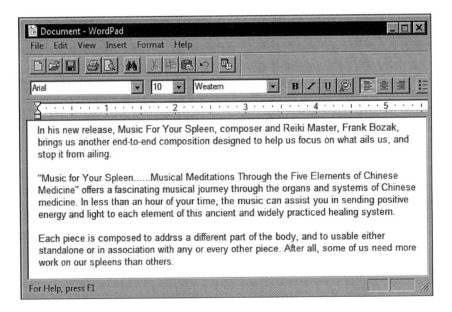

2. Copy the text.

3. Log in to the Drupal **admin** panel. Select the **Create content** option from the choices that appear, as shown in the following screenshot.

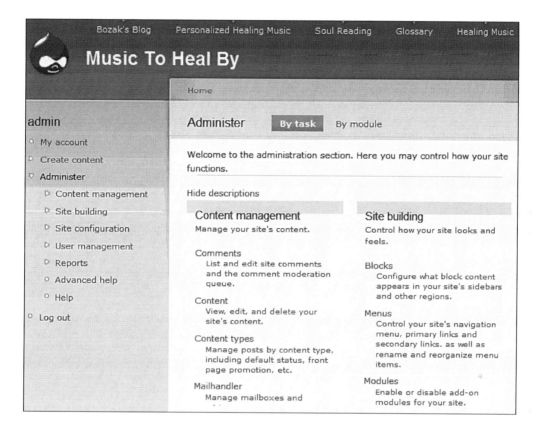

Drupal allows a theme to be set for the **admin** pages that is different from the site theme. This is a great way to avoid ever being confused about where you are. You can do this setting by selecting the **Administration theme** from the **Site configuration** menu, or by going to http://yourdomain.com/admin/settings/admin_menu.

4. The **Create content** page (seen in the upcoming screenshot) lists the Node Content types defined for the site, along with a description of each. If you're looking at the screen and wondering why it looks different, then it is because you're seeing the site theme at this point, although the admin links will still be listed in the left column as long as you are logged in. You can see this in the screenshot, and, in fact, this template being used for the site also creates a black header of admin links. It is located below the main header when on the front page, and would not be present for anyone not logged in as an **admin**. If no custom Node Content types have been added, then there will be only two types listed: **Story** and **Page**. Our project site actually has a few extra types. You're going to create a Story, so click on this link to begin.

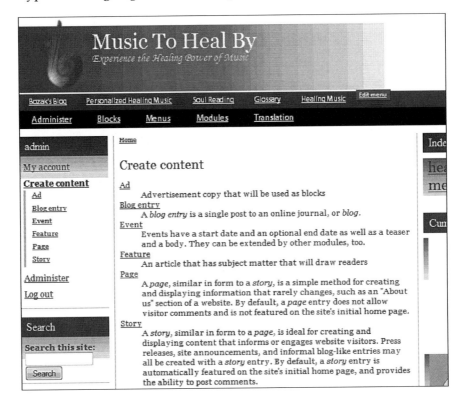

5. Having clicked on **Story**, you will see a form, as shown in the next screenshot, which you will soon come to know very well. There are a number of fields on the form that are hidden from view, and that have links to toggle their visibility. That's fine, because at this point, we only want to work with the fields that are initially visible. We'll look at them in more detail shortly. Enter the **Title** *Music For Your Spleen* in the first field (don't give it much thought; you can change it at any time).

The links and fields on your Content creation pages may vary based on the add-on modules installed and the permissions that have been granted.

Home » Create content

Create Story

Title: *

― ▸ Menu settings

Body:

― ▸ Input format

― ▸ Revision information

― ▸ Comment settings

― ▸ URL path settings

― ▸ Authoring information

― ▸ Publishing options

Save   Preview

6. The next field is the **Body**. Everything that is contained in this field becomes the page content for this Story. This is where we will paste the text that we created in the text editor. Click in the box, and then use any method that you normally use for pasting text, whether it's the browser menu, mouse click, or a keyboard shortcut. The text that we entered will now appear in the Body field. At this point you can click on the **Save** button at the bottom of the page.

You've done it! That wasn't bad at all, was it? We can now see the **Story** as a live page. Drupal automatically 'trims' the content to a certain character length, and displays it on the front page. It then inserts a link to read more, which when clicked on, takes the reader to a page where the content area is the Node Content in its entirety. The default trim length is 600 characters, but this value can be changed. In our project site, the trim length is set to 400 characters.

Changing the trim length will not affect existing content until it's edited.

The new Story will immediately appear on the front page. This is due to the default setting for Stories, which publishes them to the front page. Whenever you save Node Content, Drupal redirects you to the actual page.

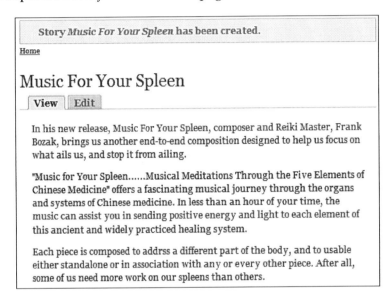

Looking at our story, there are a couple of simple formatting changes that can be made to the text in order to improve its appearance, and some minor corrections that need to be made, as well. It's time for our next activity.

Activity 2.2: Editing Node Content

We're now going to edit the story that we have just completed, and make some simple changes directly to the text. Depending on the user's permissions, the Node Content type, and other factors, editing the Node Content body will be done either in a Rich Text Editor, which we'll do in the next activity, or directly to the raw text, which we'll do now. Not all input types, Node Content types, or sites offer Rich Text editing. Therefore, learning to do it the 'old-fashioned' way is worthwhile; it is similar to learning to do long division, but much less painful.

We're still looking at the Story that we have created. Above the Story's body are two tabs (sometimes there will be more, depending on the settings): **View** and **Edit**. Click on the **Edit** tab, and the Edit page will appear with the Story in the **Body** box.

1. Let's make the corrections first:
   - Change the **F** in **For** in the title to lowercase.
   - Do the same in the first line of the body.
   - Remove the quotation marks from around the CD title in the first line of the second paragraph.
   - Change **addrss** to **address** in the first line of the final paragraph.
   - Change **to usable** to **is usable** in the same sentence.

2. We're going to italicize both instances of the CD title. Before **Music** we'll put <em>. This is an opening HTML tag. There will be a matching closing tag. Not all HTML tags come in pairs, but those that format text usually do. The <em> tag stands for emphasis, and will italicize the text following it, unless some other formatting is defined for the tag pair.

   We'll put the closing tag </em>, following **Spleen** in the first instance of the title, and another after **Medicine** in the second. Note that the slash in </em> is a forward slash.

3. We'll put a pair of tags around the artist's name too. Put <strong> before **Frank**, and </strong> after **Bozak**. If not redefined, then the <strong> tag makes the text following it bold.

4. In the following screenshot, we see the body text as it should appear after editing.

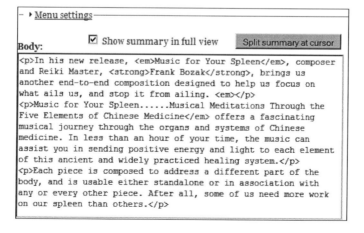

5. Click on the **Save** button, and the Story will be shown with the edits applied, as shown in next screenshot.

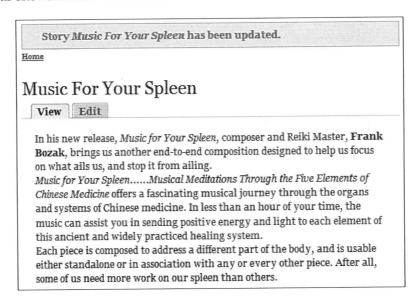

We glossed over the fields on the Content creation page before, but we should take a closer look at them before we move on to the next Node Content type and learning activity.

Content creation form fields

The form used for creating Node Content contains several links on it that, when clicked, reveal settings that you can alter. The state of these settings when you first load the page will depend on the default settings for that particular Node Content type, and whether those settings have been changed for this piece of Node Content or not. Each Node Content piece can have customized settings.

 Node Content type settings can be changed in the Content types admin area.

- **Title**: The first field is the page title. This is the only required field on the form. Once this field has an entry, you can save an empty Story or Page as a placeholder. When choosing existing Node Content to edit, use a title that you will recognize, because you will have to choose from a list of titles.

- **Menu Settings**: The menu settings are used to create a menu link to the Node Content. If you have a menu item specifically for a piece of Node Content, then you can create that link here, or, if you prefer, in the menu editor. If this piece of Node Content will be reached via other Node Content or as a front page random selection, but not via menu navigation, then these fields can remain blank.

    ◦ **Menu link title**: This is the text that will appear on the menu.

    ◦ **Parent item:** This drop-down lists all of the eligible menu items on all of the existing menus. A 'Child' menu item is an indented sub-menu choice to a 'Parent' menu item, and this item will become a child item of whichever one you select.

    ◦ **Weight**: If there are other Child items for the Parent item that you select, then these will appear in alphabetical order with other items of the same weight. 'Weight' is simply a numerical value, and if the items are sorted by weight rather than by, let's say, name or by creation date, then they will appear in the order that the weight values determine.

- **Body**: The text and tags that comprise the content.

- **Input format**: The input formats dictate which HTML tags are usable for input, and the filtering and actions that are performed (when the content is displayed) to enforce them. They are defined on the admin **Input formats** page, which is part of the **Site configuration** section. Input formats can be allowed or disallowed for specific user types. There are three pre-loaded types of input, of which the first two are enabled by default.

    ◦ **Filtered HTML** (default): This filters out all but the most basic HTML tags, thus allowing only basic formatting of the content.

    ◦ **Full HTML**: This input type allows all HTML tags, and thus enables the highest level of formatting.

    ◦ **PHP Code**: This is enabled if the **PHP filter** module is activated. It allows PHP script snippets to be inserted into the content. This, in turn, provides access to the system variables, as well as to content that is external to Drupal.

 PHP input should only be allowed for trusted programming experts. Not only can it accidentally damage the layout, but also when abused intentionally, it can destroy your site.

- **Revision information**: This is used in a similar fashion to a word processing program, to create a revised version of an article, and to record comments about the revision for other content creators to see.

- **Comment settings:** This determines whether site users will be able to submit comments about this Node Content. Depending on your settings, submitted comments will either be displayed immediately or only following an approval.
  - **Disabled:** There will be no comment link shown
  - **Read Only**: Existing comments will be displayed
  - **Read/Write:** New comments will be accepted

- **URL Path Settings**: This is present because the **Path** module has been activated. The contents of this field will be used as the URL for this Node Content. Using this feature requires that the Mod-Rewrite option be enabled and configured for your Web domain. These paths are considered 'friendly' URLs, because they are much more meaningful to the site visitor, and are usable by search engines, because they will often contain terms related to the content, rather than identification numbers, and so on.

- **Authoring information**: This stores information about the author of the Node Content, and will be displayed if the site is configured accordingly. This setting can be changed in the **Global settings** section of the **admin | Themes** page.
  - **Authored by**: This contains the username of the author of the Node Content. This field will default to the user creating the Node Content. Often, Node Content is created on behalf of someone else. The user name *can* be changed. This field has auto-complete enabled, so you only need to type the first character or two of the username. Leave the field blank to have an *anonymous* author.
  - **Authored on**: This defaults to the date and time that the Node Content was created, but can be overridden. This information will be used for sorting in relation to other Node Content, as with, let's say, blog entries.

- **Publishing options**: These options specify how the Node Content is used.
  - **Published:** The Node Content will be available to be viewed.
  - **Promoted to front page:** The Node Content is available to be selected as material for the front page, and will appear there if it is newer than other promoted Content.
  - **Stick at top of lists**: The Content will remain at the top of the lists of Node Content, such as on the front page.

Node Content types—Page

If having 'content' as a keyword in Drupal isn't confusing enough, then how about Page also being a keyword? To avoid confusion in our work, we'll capitalize the word, when it is being used in the Drupal context and not to mean a generic page.

Drupal looks at a Page as being Node Content that will not be published automatically in the Node Content area of the front page, as the story that we just created was. Instead, it sees the Page as being something that is, perhaps, relatively static, such as an **About Us** page. The default Publication settings for a Page reflect this, as the **Promoted to front page** option is not selected.

That said, there is no real difference between a Story and a Page. In fact, you are free to change the default settings for either Node Content type so that there is no difference at all, or, for example, so that a Story acts like a Page, and a Page like a Story. Even by leaving the default settings as they are, you can choose to (un)publish or (un)promote a piece of Node Content at any time, via the admin panel or by editing it.

Now, let's create a Page for the site.

Activity 2.3: Creating a Drupal Page with a Rich Text Editor

We're going to use a **Rich Text Editor** (RTE). Drupal doesn't come with one installed, so we asked our site administrator to install one (this is not a task for non-administrator types) and he chose FCKeditor by Frederico Caldeira Knabben.

1. From the screen we were last on, click on the **Create content** link.
2. On the node add page, choose the Node Content type **Page**.
3. The **Create content** form for Page is the same as the one for Story. We'll start by adding a **Title** of **Personalized Healing Music**.
4. With this Node Content, we will need a menu link. Let's click on the **Menu settings** button to open up the menu dialog.
5. In the **Menu link title** field, we'll enter the title **Personalized Healing Music** again.

6. In the **Parent item** drop-down list, we'll select the **<Primary links>** option, which is near the bottom of the list. Our menu settings now look similar to those shown in the following screenshot.

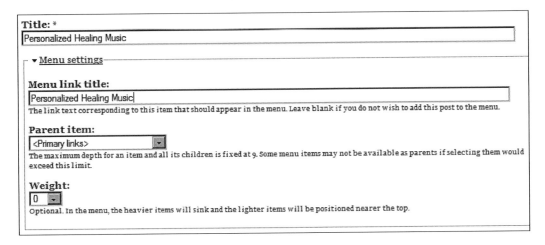

7. Click on the link below the body box that says **Switch to Rich Text Editor**. The FCKeditor toolbar appears above it, as seen in the following screenshot.

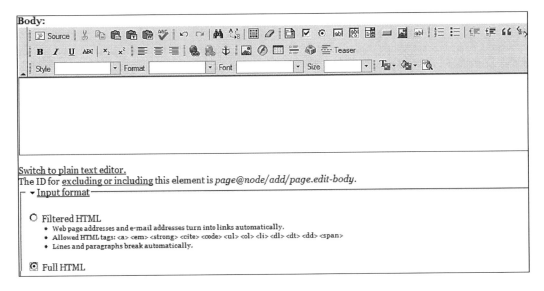

8. Click on the **Input format** link, which is below the box, and choose the **Full HTML** option. We don't want our entry to be filtered.

The available functions (buttons) are configurable, so your implementation may look somewhat different.

Some people prefer to format text as they are typing. Others, like me, prefer to enter the text first, and then format it. Use whichever technique you are most comfortable with. The instructions in this example will assume that you've entered the text first. The screenshot shows the unformatted text, as it will appear after typing in the **Body** box. Feel free to type as much as you want.

The harnessed power of music is one of the oldest and strongest forces in the universe. Allowing the energy of music to restore a body to its natural state is using music in its most honorable form. Music's energy flowing through your body can root out any negative energy, then bring you back to a state of renewed health, harmony and peace.

Like other forms of energy, music is composed of vibrations. If you consider your body as a pool of water, the vibrations of the music first skim the water, gently removing any debris on the surface. Then, it begins to churn, drawing debris from the depths to the surface. There, the vibrations break up the debris and sweep it away, until the surface of the water is smooth.

By using my gifts as a composer and Reiki Master, I create music that has the power to transform and to heal. The music will gently lead you on to the next step in life.

In films, music is used to follow and enhance the sights on the screen, and as a subtle clue as to what lies next. I treat the evolution of your soul as a film, scoring the imagery being shown to me, and offering subtle clues as to what lies next. A new musical idea is created from each aspect of your soul. Each of these new ideas are created from the original seed of thought. And each one offers clues and insights into what comes next.

Many of you have paid $250 for a psychic reading, and within a week or two, no longer remember what was said to you. Your music will last for the rest of your life

There is no resale of this music by me. It is totally yours. I will ask you to not to sell or distribute it to any one at all. I have found that ten to twelve minutes of music seems to be the best time length. It is long enough to capture your attention, and short enough to not interrupt your day. With these optimal conditions you will be apt to continue listening on a recurring basis.

Sometimes the actual composing comes quickly, sometimes it takes a few weeks. The cost for your music is $350.00 USD. Click here and complete a simple form to begin your composition. Due to the complexity of the project, please allow four to six weeks to complete the personal soundtrack of your soul.

9. With your text entered, the first change we'll make is to make it a little larger. Click on the **Select All** button. This selects all of your text.

10. With all of the text selected, simply click on the down arrow on the **Size** box, and select **larger**.

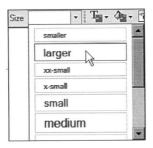

11. Highlight the word **gently** in the second sentence of the second paragraph, and then click on the Italicize button.

12. Later in the final paragraph, we'll be adding a link to the word **here**, after the price. For now, we'll just make the text blue as a reminder. Highlight the word, and then click on the Text color button and select the middle blue square, as shown in the example below.

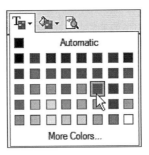

13. Open the **Publishing options** dialog, and promote the Page, so that we will get a 'teaser' on the front page.

14. **Save** what we've done. We can now see the finished Page. Now, let's log off, and see the front page as a visitor will see it, with our new teaser and menu link, as shown in the next screenshot.

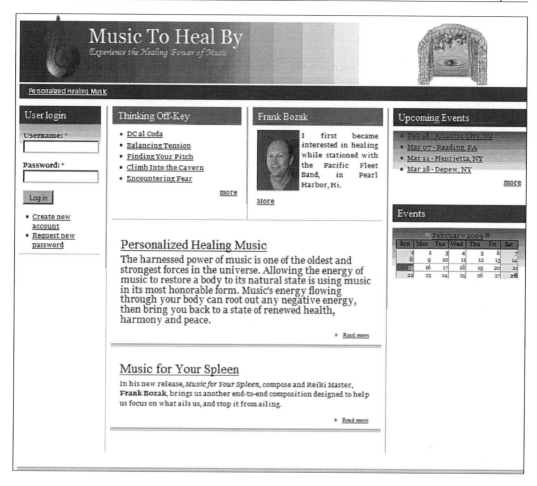

Permissions in Drupal

A quick discussion of Drupal's permissions system is in order. In this chapter's activities, we were able to create and edit as we liked. This was possible because we were logged in as the owner, who, by default, has permissions to do anything.

Later on, we will take a close look and perform an activity with regards to workflow, which involves users, their roles, and the associated permissions. For now, let's note that there are permissions that can be allowed or denied, and that certain permission types apply to what we have done. They are listed as follows:

- Create [Node] Content
- Edit one's own Content

- Edit the [Node] Content of others
- Use the Rich Text Editor
- Administer Content
- Administer Nodes

Summary

We have learned about Node Content in this chapter. This chapter has also taught us:

- What Drupal considers to be Content (the difference between 'content' and 'Node Content')
- The two principal types of Node Content, namely Story and Page
- How to create a Story
- How to create a Page
- What the fields on the Content creation form are used for
- How to create Node Content using pasted text
- How to create Node Content using raw text
- How to create and format Node Content using the Rich Text Editor
- How to insert HTML into raw text
- What the permissions associated with Node Content are

In Chapter 3, we will look at adding a little spice to our Node Content, by using the types of Rich Content that you and your site visitors have come to expect from web sites.

3
Content Seasoning

In the previous chapter, we learned about the creation of Pages and Stories: Node Content. Certainly, adding articles and pages to your site is paramount, but site visitors don't live by text alone.

Just like a chicken recipe becomes an entirely new meal when treated with Thai or Indian spices (to name two), a web site also needs some spicing up. Of course, recognizing the need for some seasoning, and applying the ingredients, are two different things. So, let's learn to season our Node Content.

What you will learn

In this chapter, you will learn to:

- Display 'teasers' (excerpts) — much like a newspaper's front page
- Link to other Node Content — the Read More link that you see on many web sites
- Use images
- Add audio and video — to add richness to your page content
- Link to downloadable content such as PDF files — to add value to your site

What you will do

In this chapter, you will be:

- Adding a teaser to the front page
- Linking to other Node Content
- Inserting an image
- Embedding a music clip
- Adding a video

Understanding Teasers

There is a limited amount of space available on a web page. It may not seem that way, as you can scroll down. However, it's one thing to scroll down when scanning images on a web site for a product that you want, and another when reading content. Most visitors will not sit and read an endless page; they'll 'bounce'. This is the term used to describe the act of navigating away from your site, and that is something that you don't want to happen.

A solution is to create a small article, a **Story**, that contains a reference to, or subset of, the original piece in the form of a Read More link. A **Teaser** is when you show enough Node Content to create an interest in the remainder of the Story. Drupal allows you to determine exactly how much Node Content you want to show. Essentially, you are putting a 'mark' in the Page or Story. This way, you can have a five-paragraph Story, but only display one paragraph on the front page. There aren't two versions or copies of the piece, just a tag, which tells Drupal where to provide a link to the remainder of the Node Content.

Unfortunately, you cannot define where in the piece to begin. That is, a teaser always shows Node Content from the beginning up to the place where you've indicated.

The question arises then, "what connects this excerpt with the original?" — Drupal does. It provides a link to **Read more**, which takes the visitor to a page containing the entire original Node Content.

So let's create a Teaser.

Activity 3.1: Creating a Teaser

In this activity, we'll create some Page content with a teaser.

1. Go to the **Create content** page, and select **Page** as the Node Content type.

2. The following screenshot shows the Page fields, containing content. Copy it or create your own, but have at least two paragraphs, so that there is a difference between the full Page and the excerpted teaser.

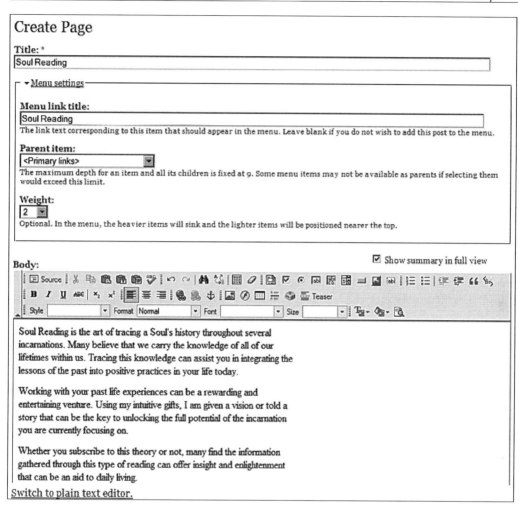

3. Since we have the RTE panel active, we'll use the editor to create the teaser break. We're using FCKeditor, in this example, and its teaser break button.

4. Place the cursor before the first word of the second paragraph, and click on the **Insert Teaser Break** button. You will see a separator appear. Everything above this separator will appear both in the teaser on the front page, and in the full article. Everything below the separator will not appear in the teaser.

> Soul Reading is the art of tracing a Soul's history throughout several incarnations. Many believe that we carry the knowledge of all of our lifetimes within us. Tracing this knowledge can assist you in integrating the
>
> lessons of the past into positive practices in your life today.
>
> ---
>
> Working with your past life experiences can be a rewarding and entertaining venture. Using my intuitive gifts, I am given a vision or told a story that can be the key to unlocking the full potential of the incarnation you are currently focusing on.
>
> Whether you subscribe to this theory or not, many find the information gathered through this type of reading can offer insight and enlightenment that can be an aid to daily living.

5. Now that we have created a teaser, let's take a look at how to create one when not using the editor. Simply click on the **Switch to plain text editor** link below the body box. This will turn off the editor. The body box will now become two boxes: one that shows the teaser, and one that shows the rest. You will notice a **Join Summary** button. Clicking on it will remove the teaser break. If there were no teaser present, then the button would read **Split summary at cursor**, and clicking on it would create the teaser break. Try it!

☑ Show summary in full view   Join summary

Body:

```
<p>Soul Reading is the art of tracing a Soul's history throughout several<br />
incarnations. Many believe that we carry the knowledge of all of our<br />
lifetimes within us. Tracing this knowledge can assist you in integrating the<br />
lessons of the past into positive practices in your life today.</p>
```

```
<p>Working with your past life experiences can be a rewarding and<br />
entertaining venture. Using my intuitive gifts, I am given a vision or told a<br />
story that can be the key to unlocking the full potential of the incarnation<br />
you are currently focusing on.</p>
<p>Whether you subscribe to this theory or not, many find the information<br />
gathered through this type of reading can offer insight and enlightenment<br />
that can be an aid to daily living.</p>
```

6. Under the **Publishing options** heading, click on the **Promote to front page** box. Drupal will then display the teaser on the front page.

7. **Save** the new Page. Drupal will present the Page in its entirety. Note the new menu choice in the top navigation bar.

8. The final thing to do is to view the Page as a teaser. Click on the **Home** link above the Page title, and you will see that the first paragraph of our new Page appears as a teaser in the top content area of the front page, along with a link to read the rest of the article.

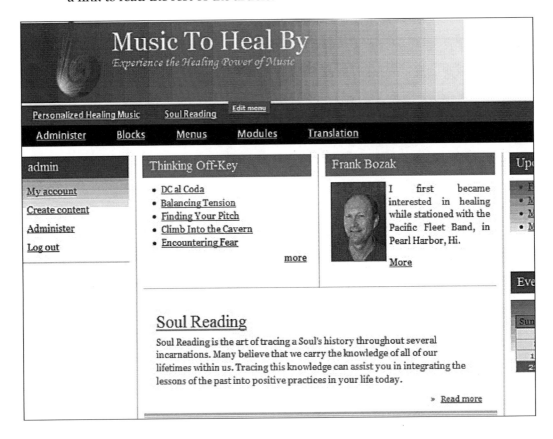

If you decide to remove a Page or Story teaser from the front page, then instead of just waiting for newer Node Content to displace it, all you need to do is edit the Node Content and clear the **Promote to front page** box. If your intent is to still have the Node Content available for reading in its entirety, then make sure that there's a link to it someplace on your site.

The result of a teaser break is much like the automatic trimming that Drupal does, based on the settings, as we saw earlier. The difference is that with a teaser break, you control precisely what is shown in the teaser. With automatic trimming, there is no such precision.

How do you place a teaser break in Pages and Stories that are not meant for the front page? How do you create the same mechanism in content other than Pages and Stories? Great questions! In these cases, Drupal does not necessarily provide a teaser mechanism. You may need to create a **pseudo teaser break** by having to separate pieces of content, and then use a link to connect one to the other.

We're going to look at the links next, and we'll do an activity to create a 'pseudo teaser break' later in the chapter.

At this point of time, it is not uncommon to run into issues with Rich Text Editors in Drupal that do not properly support teaser breaks. In the FCKeditor that we are using, the teaser break is supported properly, but the button is not available in the default installation, and needs to be enabled. If you are using an editor with no **Insert Teaser Break** button or with one that doesn't function properly, then you can try editing the text raw (turn off the editor). If you find that the **Split Summary at Cursor** button is missing, try inserting `<!--break-->` (formatted exactly with two hyphens following the ! and two before the >) in your text where you want the break to appear. Note that you might have to disengage the editor whenever using the page containing this text, as it might consider the tag invalid and deactivate it.

Creating links within Node Content

Like anyone who uses the Internet, you are undoubtedly familiar with links. These words, typically blue and underlined, and sometimes images, link one web page to another.

There are several destination types for which a link is useful:

1. Content intended to be downloaded—for example, a PDF file of the complete catalog of recordings.
2. Video or audio content—such as a music clip from a CD.
3. Pages elsewhere on the Web—reviews, for example.
4. Page content within your own web site—such as a shopping cart for purchases.

We will address all four types within this chapter. Let's begin with the fundamentals of what a link is and how it is constructed.

Activity 3.2: Creating an external text link

We're going to edit the Node Content that we already have, and add a text link to another web site to it.

1. Navigate to the Content management page, via the admin links, or simply append `admin/content/node` to the domain name to get there.

Navigating within Drupal

The link that we have just seen is a shortcut to the admin page function, rather than clicking through a series of menus. Each word represents a choice from one of the menu levels (**Admin | Manage content | Content**), although the choice of words, as here, is not always intuitive. Take note of the link showing in your browser's address bar when you're on the admin pages, and soon you'll begin to remember them. Here is a list of some of the ones used most often:

`admin/content/node` — edit content

`admin/content/node/add` — create content

`admin/build/block` — create and edit blocks

`admin/build/views` — create and edit views

2. Click on the **Edit** button for the **Music for Your Spleen** Story.
3. If the RTE is not visible, then click on the **Switch to rich text editor** option.
4. Find the word **Reiki** in the first line, and select it with your mouse.
5. Click on the **Insert/Edit Link** button.

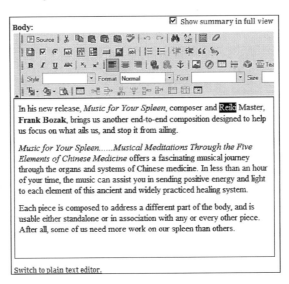

6. This will bring up the FCKeditor's Link dialog box. Enter **ReikiHealingHands.net** in the **URL** box.

7. Click on the **Target** tab and pick **New Window** from the **Target** drop-down box. This opens a new window (or tab, depending on the site visitor's browser settings) when the link is clicked, so that visitors don't leave our site.

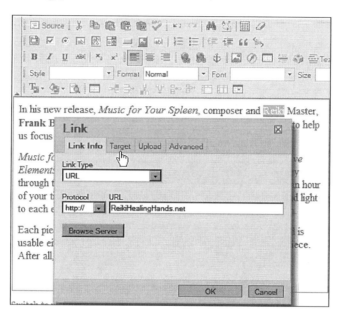

8. Click on the **OK** button, and we now have a link in our body text.

9. The link is fully-functional, but there is something else we need to add to it. However, the editor does not offer the setting that we need, so we'll have to make the change manually. Let's turn off the editor, by clicking on the **Switch to plain text editor** option below the body box. This gives us the raw text and shows the HTML tags.

10. We're going to edit the link tag, which appears highlighted in the upcoming screenshot, but not on the screen.

11. We put our cursor immediately before the closing bracket in **="blank">Reiki** and add a space and **rel="nofollow"**. The modified link should now read:

```
<a href="http://ReikiHealingHands.net" target="_blank"
                  rel="nofollow">
```

The `target=` parameter allows you to control how the linked page will be shown. Here we use `_blank`, which specifies that the page should appear on its own window or tab. This is a good practice when you want to show additional content, but do not want to send the visitor away from your site.

To follow—or not to follow

`rel="nofollow"` tells the 'spiders' that are sent out by the search engines in order to index the Web, to not proceed to the site named in the link. We want to have a link to that site, but don't want its contents used to rank ours. If the link is to content that you have no control over, then it's best to use the `"nofollow"` parameter.

12. Click on the **Save** button at the bottom of the screen, and we're done.

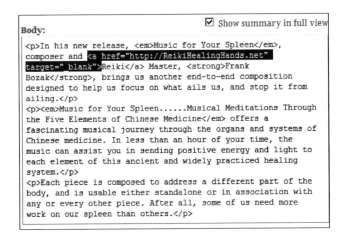

The anatomy of a link

Links are one of the oldest pieces of HTML, and long predate the **World Wide Web**. Originally, the Internet was used by government and education researchers as a tool. Even before the need for, or the existence of, video and MP3s, and before the need for precise and eye-catching screen layouts, there was the need for being able to move between pieces of content. Thus was created the **hyperlink**, or simply, a link.

Links can be text links, where some text is used to link to another location, or image links, where an image or button accomplishes the same. Let's take a look at a typical text link.

```
<a href="http://www.mydomain.com/index.html">Click here</a>
```

If not overridden by other formatting, then this link would appear as: **Click here**.

The <a> </a> pair surround the text that is to be the clickable link. href stands for **hyperlink reference**, and this is the address that will be requested when the link is clicked on. The reference is a URL or a URI. The difference is that an external site must be a fully-qualified Web address containing http:// or https://. An address local to the site can just be a page name (or other content) like index.html. **Universal Resource Locater (URL)** and **Universal Resource Identifier (URI)** are not completely the same, although they tend to be used interchangeably. Something like http://mydomain.com is a URL; it is used to locate the resource mydomain.com. All URLs are URIs, but URIs are not always URLs.

Using images in content

"A picture's worth a thousand words"

Even though this saying pre-dates the Internet, it still applies today. However, with 'inflation' on the rise, it's probably more like 100 words, or about twenty or so lines in a column, which is as much as you want to have without some kind of image to hold the reader's attention.

Inserting links into images in content so that the image referenced by the link will be shown, is fairly simple to do in Drupal. However, uploading the image file into a directory on the server where the web site is located can be a challenge. But don't worry; I'm here to help. The challenge is getting the upload service configured properly, and that's the administrator's job, not yours. Once configured, the upload is simple.

If your site doesn't have an editor or a module that provides uploading (FCKeditor does, as long as the upload service is enabled), then you'll need to resort to something more manual, such as **FTP (File Transfer Protocol)**.

Let's add an image to our Node Content.

Activity 3.3: Working with images in content

In this activity, we will do a number of things with regards to image content, and so we'll divide it into two sub-activities:

- Uploading and embedding an image
- Creating an image link

Activity 3.3a: Uploading and embedding an image

The specifics of uploading will vary with the tool being used. In this example, we'll use the upload functionality of IMCE, an image-uploading add-on to the Rich Text Editor that we're using.

1. Let's re-edit the same content that we used in the *Creating a teaser break* activity, and make sure that the editor is activated.

2. We want the image to be at the beginning of the text, so place the cursor there, and then click on the **Insert/Edit Image** button.

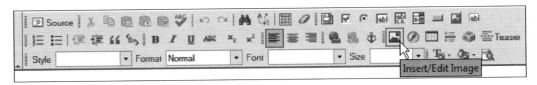

3. The **Image Properties** dialog box appears. At this point, we can name an image, or browse to it, if it is already on the server. As a prerequisite, our image has to be uploaded, so click on the **Upload** tab.

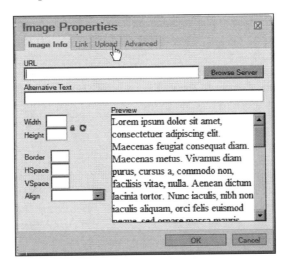

4. Assume that the image to be uploaded is located in the c:\temp folder. We'll click on the **Browse** button, navigate to the image, and then click on the **Send it to the Server** button.

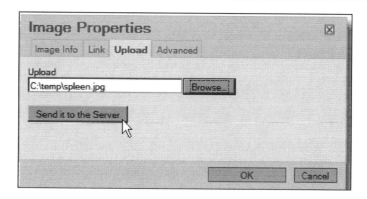

5. If all goes well, then a success message similar to the following screenshot will be displayed. The image file will be deposited in a directory on the server. Drupal will have been configured to use the directory for uploads, and therefore will also know that it has to look in that directory when we wish to select an image.

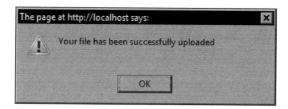

6. We are now returned to the **Image Info** tab. The file's **URL** and dimensions have been filled in for us, and a thumbnail is also provided.

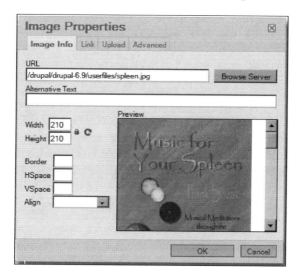

7. We will now add some additional information. We will set the **Border** to **0** (this will prevent a blue box from appearing around the image when we make it a link) and **Align** it to the **Right**. Putting some descriptive text in the **Alternative Text** field helps with **Search Engine Optimization (SEO)**, which is the manipulation that you can do to web site content in order to (hopefully) achieve a higher placement in search results.

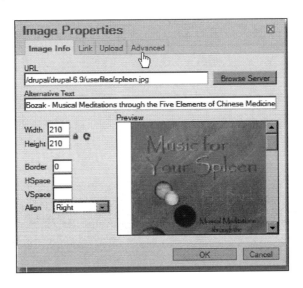

8. Next, click on the **Advanced** tab. In the **Advanced** settings, enter the following text into the **Style** box:

```
padding: 0 0 3px 3px
```

This will set some whitespace between the text and the bottom and left edges of the image.

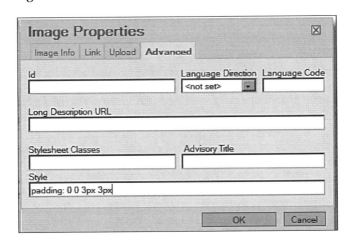

The line of code that we just saw is **Cascading Style Sheet (CSS)** code. Originally, positioning of all of the elements on a web page were done using **Hyper Text Markup Language (HTML)**, as well as the formatting of those elements (type size, button colors, and so on). It became very difficult to maintain with everything mixed together, not to mention that pages that were similar, had the same HTML repeated again and again with a minor change needed in many places. CSS allows positioning and formatting to be separated from the page HTML, as rules, and referred to indirectly. Therefore, for example, if you want 12-point text that is blue anywhere, then you can have a rule defined once, and then simply refer to it.

9. Click on the **OK** button, and the image now becomes part of the body text.

10. At this point we can save the Node Content. After doing so, return to the front page, and you will see the image in our Teaser.

That's it for this activity. We've successfully uploaded and added an image to our content using the Rich Text Editor. But what if you don't have a RTE? Not a problem! The editor simply adds an HTML tag to the body text for you.

Inserting an image if you don't have an editor

Even if you do not have a Rich Text Editor, you will still need to transfer the image onto the server so that you can use it. Ask your site administrator about uploading the file using FTP. Once it has been uploaded, you just need to know its location within the web site. For example, if the file is `myimage.jpg`, then its location might be `images/myimage.jpg`. Your site administrator can help you with that, too.

Once you have the file in place, simply add the HTML tag into your body text just before the paragraph that you want it next to. Here is the simplest form of the tag, without the alternate text, border, or spacing options added. Note that the tag is standalone, and not in pairs as was the `<a>` tag earlier.

```
<img src="/images/myimage.jpg" />
```

In the example above, `img` stands for *image*, `src` stands for the *source* of the image, and the final / is there because this is a standalone tag.

A tag containing all of the options we chose as well as the information that Drupal provided automatically, looks like this:

```
<img height="210" width="210" border="0" align="right"
src="/images/myimage.jpg" alt="some alternate text here" />
```

This is an example of HTML. For the most part, HTML is composed of 'tags', information within angled brackets < > that define the content of a web page. Here, `border` is the size of the image border in pixels (in this case, none), and `align` defines on which side of the text the image should be aligned. `alt` is the text to be shown if the image cannot be found, or if the page is being displayed to someone who has chosen not to receive images. For example, a Text-to-Speech system can give a visually-impaired site visitor a description of what is present on the site. The `height` and `width` are the dimensions of the image, in pixels. The image will be shown at its original size if the dimensions are not specified. Having the dimensions set speeds up the page load, because the browser knows in advance how much space to set aside.

Activity 3.3b: Creating an image link

Now that we have an image in our text, let's use it as a link. Any image can be used as a link. Sometimes you may want to have a nice graphic for the reader to click on, instead of a text link or a standard button. On sites where images are links to themselves, such as in photo galleries, the image link might be a small 'thumbnail' that, when clicked on, leads to a full-sized version of the image. Internet users are used to images often being clickable. Here's how to do create such a link:

1. Re-edit the Node Content in which we just added the image.

2. If necessary, activate your editor. We'll use FCKeditor for our example.

3. In the **Body** box, click on the image once. Clicking on the image will cause handles to appear around it, as seen in the following screenshot.

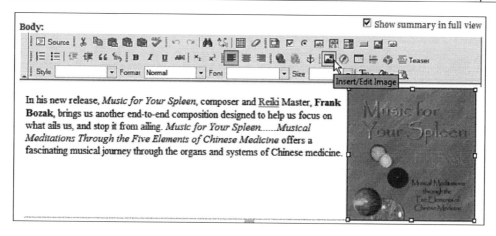

4. Click on the **Insert/Edit Image** button.

5. The **Image Properties** pop-up box will appear. Click on the **Link** tab.

6. We're going to link the image to the full (non-teaser) version of the article for now. We can change the 'target' later, when we have more content. We'll enter **/node/15** into the **URL** field, and then click on the **OK** button.

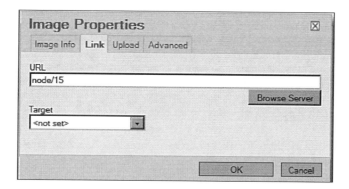

7. **Save** the Node Content, and then navigate to the front page and click on the image.

At the time of writing, the FCKeditor did not provide browse functionality to select Node Content for linking, so a link to the Node Content needs to be entered. The required link is the portion of the URL (when viewing the full Node Content) that follows the domain name. Therefore, with a URL of `http://mydomain.com/node/15`, the link would be `/node/15`. Every piece of Node Content has a node ID in the form of a number. There are two easy ways to find this number. One is to look below the **Body** box when editing the Content. The URL will be listed there. The other way is go to the screen where all of the Node Content is listed (`admin/content/node`), and hold your mouse over the name of your Node Content, which on that page will be a link. Your browser will show the URL assigned to the link, and this will contain the node number.

Embedding audio in Node Content

Audio content on your website can surely act as an "attention grabber". Not only does it provide an interface where portraying text can be difficult, but it also provides a means of enhancing a presentation or entertaining your web site's visitors.

Activity 3.4: Adding audio content

We're going to add an audio clip to the Node Content that we've been working with in this chapter. Neither Drupal nor the FCKeditor provides a specific method for uploading a music file. FCKeditor is clueless about the player that we choose to use, and so has no way of generating the code needed to embed the file. With images, all that is needed is an HTML image tag. With audio and video files, it's more complex. The audio file for this activity is already on the server, but how would you get the file onto your server?

Uploading audio files to the server

If the ultimate location for the audio files on your site should be the same as for the images, then simply follow the instructions that we have just seen for uploading an image file until the file has been uploaded. Then cancel out of the Image dialog box (that is, don't try to use it to embed the file). If the location needs to be different, and if there is no upload facility installed, then you will need to use FTP.

Let's embed the audio file in our Node Content.

1. Re-edit the **Music for Your Spleen** Node Content.

2. The clip is going to be placed at the end of the current text, so go to the very end of it and enter the following text on a new line:

   Click here to play a clip from the track Lungs

3. We're not going to use the editor for the next part, so turn it off by clicking on the **Switch to plain text** option below the **Body** box.

4. Add a space after "Lungs", and then type the following:

   ```
   <swf file="music/Lungs.mp3"></swf>
   ```

5. **Save** the Node Content, and you will see the player.

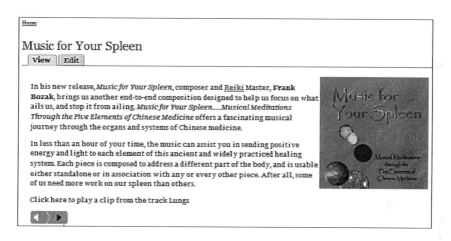

6. Click on the play metaphor (arrow), and the player will expand and begin playing the audio file.

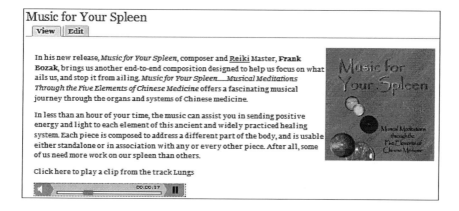

The tag that we entered is specific, in content and in format, to the use of the **SWF Tools** module and the type of audio file that we used. Embedding tags used for audio and video within a Content Management System typically does not use standard HTML. This activity gives you a good idea of the process involved, even though the specifics will vary.

Adding sound to a page can be complicated. There are several pieces that need to align (including the proper stars and planets!). There are different file formats for audio, and each has different requirements with regard to the software needed to:

- Play the music
- Provide the on-screen player
- Connect the two to the browser
- Connect all of the above-mentioned points to the Drupal framework

The main issue to be resolved is "what is supported in Drupal?". One of the most popular formats for playing music online (and in a hand-held player) is MP3. Drupal supports MP3 playback by way of an add-on module called **SWF Tools**. SWF is a file format associated with Flash videos, but this module will also handle MP3 audio. This test site uses the **SWF Tools** module. The next thing is the player itself; what does the visitor see on the screen? The **SWF Tools** module provides a generic player in the form of a play arrow, and it also provides support for some third-party players. In this project site, the player is **1 Pixel Out**, a popular third-party player.

The installation, configuration, and testing of the pieces needed for supporting audio files is not for the layman or for the faint-hearted. My recommendation is that if your site is not already set up to handle audio files, then have your site administrator install this capability. If support has already been provided, then ask three questions to your administrator:

- What formats can you use (MP3, for example)?
- In which directory on the server should you put the files?
- How do you embed the file within your content?

Audio files can be a great addition to your Node Content. However, I would recommend against having them play automatically. This is because site visitors are often sitting at their desk at work and loathe having their computer draw the attention of their co-workers.

Linking to downloadable content

As we saw earlier, another use of links is to provide a link to content, such as a PDF file, that can be downloaded. In this way, you can provide value-added documents to your site visitor. The more useful content you can provide, the more the search engines will 'like' your site, and the more people will use it. With our site, the site owner might want to provide a printable catalog, or bonus material for people who buy one of his CDs.

Activity 3.5: Providing a link to downloadable content

In this activity, we will use some of the techniques that we learned earlier in the chapter, and create a link in our Node Content for the visitor to download a PDF file. We're going to use an image as the link.

1. Navigate to and edit the **Soul Reading** Node Content.

2. Ensure that your text editor is activated.

3. Go to the end of the article, and add a new line.

4. Click on the **Insert/Edit Image** button.

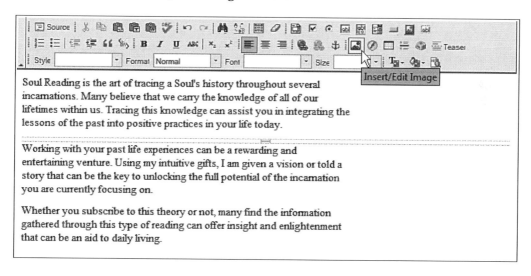

5. Next, click on the **Browse** button.

6. On the Browse screen, we will click on the `pdf.gif` file name.

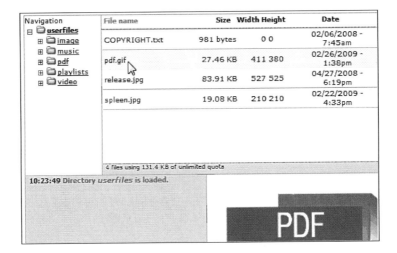

7. With the image file selected, we'll click on the **Send to FCKEditor** button.

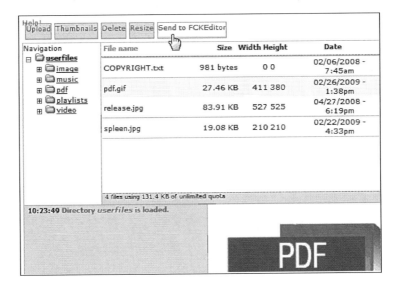

8. Back in the **Image Properties** dialog, we will change the **Width** setting to **82**, which in turn automatically changes the **Height** setting to **76**, because the proportions are maintained.

9. We'll enter a value of **0** in the **Border** size setting, so that the link doesn't have a blue box around it.

10. Finally, we enter the **Alternative Text** as **Download the Soul Reading pdf**.

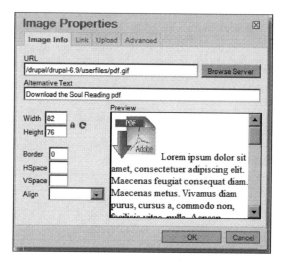

11. At this point, we can click on the **Link** tab, and browse to the file that we are linking to. However, at the time of writing, this method didn't work dependably, so we will click on the **OK** button, and create the link separately.

12. Click on the **Insert/Edit Link** button.

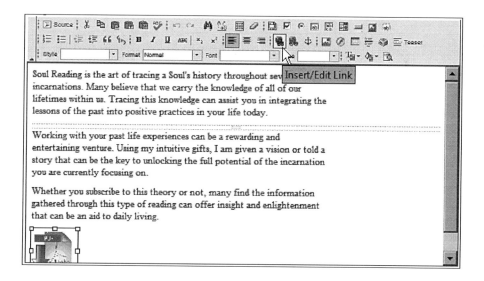

13. On the link pop-up, we'll click on the **Browse** button.

14. In the Browse window, we'll select the pdf folder. Note that what we select here depends on the location of the files on our server. It is very likely that the files may be stored at a different location on your server, when compared to the example below.

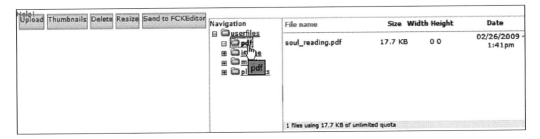

15. We'll click the file **soul_reading.pdf**, and this will cause the file name to appear in the bottom pane as a link, which we will click on.

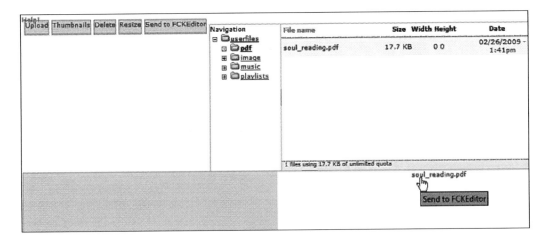

16. The **Link** window now contains the **URL** of our PDF file. We can now click on the **OK** button.

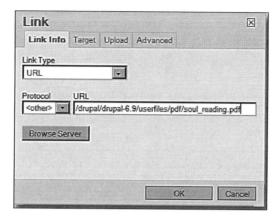

Voilà! We have our finished Node Content, with an image link, which, when clicked on, will either load the PDF file or download it, depending on the visitor's browser. When creating a link for downloadable material, such as this one, it's best to set `target="_blank"`, as we discussed earlier. This way a new browser window or tab will be used.

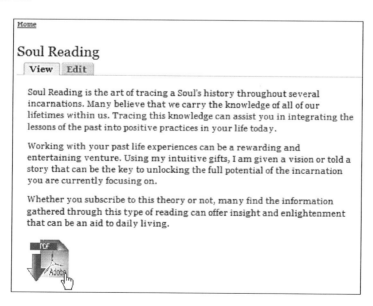

Embedding video in Node Content

The discussion in the preceding section, *Embedding audio in Node Content*, regarding the complexities of embedding audio content, will double for video content as well. The differences between video contents like **Flash** and **Quicktime** might not only make the player and supporting software different, but also affect the parameters needed to play the content. Some video player modules, such as SWF (the one we're using), can handle several types of content. Parameters such as the width and height of the player are usually supported for any video content, but additional options (background color, buttons on the player, and more) vary greatly.

We will be using the simple video viewer that comes with the SWF Tools module. This has no controls, and will start playing the video as soon as the page loads. More advanced video players, with pause, mute, and play controls, can be installed if your site requires it. Certainly, if you will have a page with several videos available for viewing, then you won't want them all to start playing when the page loads!

Activity 3.6: Adding video content

As we already have the **SWF Tools** module installed, we'll add a Flash video file (`.flv`) to our Node Content. We can just as easily add QuickTime or other supported formats; the process is the same.

Let's embed the Flash movie in our Node Content.

1. Re-edit the **Music for Your Spleen** Node Content.

2. The clip is going to be at the end of the current text, so go to the very end of it and enter the following code on a new line:

   ```
   <swf file="video/video.flv"></swf>
   ```

3. **Save** your Node Content, and you will see the movie , as shown in the following example.

In his new release, *Music for Your Spleen*, composer and <u>Reiki</u> Master, **Frank Bozak**, brings us another end-to-end composition designed to help us focus on what ails us, and stop it from ailing. *Music for Your Spleen......Musical Meditations Through the Five Elements of Chinese Medicine* offers a fascinating musical journey through the organs and systems of Chinese medicine.

In less than an hour of your time, the music can assist you in sending positive energy and light to each element of this ancient and widely practiced healing system. Each piece is composed to address a different part of the body, and is usable either standalone or in association with any or every other piece. After all, some of us need more work on our spleen than others.

Click here to play a clip from the track Lungs

The tag that we entered is specific, in content and in format, to the use of the **SWF Tools** module and the type of video file that we used. Embedding tags used for audio and video within a Content Management System typically does not use standard HTML. This activity gives you a good idea of the process involved, even though the specifics will vary. Lucky for us, the module worries about those specifics, so we don't have to.

Summary

This chapter covered the following topics:

- What a teaser is, and how you can squeeze more content offering onto your front page by using one
- Creating teasers in various ways
- Linking within your site and outside your site, so that your visitors can quickly navigate to the information that interests them
- Embedding images, audio, and video within your Node Content to add richness, variety, and a more pleasing experience for your visitors
- Creating an image link to add more functionality to images, because visitors are used to clicking on images linking to something
- Using a link for a file download (a `.pdf` file in our activity), which provides value-added content to your site visitor

In Chapter 4, we will perform some more advanced editing of content using HTML and PHP, and will also learn about working with revisions.

4
Advanced Content Editing

In the previous chapters, we have learned how to create Node Content and apply minor editing to it. The level of control over the appearance of the text that we saw is fine if only some basic changes are called for (such as underlining a word here, making a word bold there, while retaining the default top-down paragraph style). However that's not always the case. Sometimes you may need to do something different that requires some customization to your Node Content, or perhaps to instances of similar Node Content.

Aside from the requirements affecting appearance, there are also times when a Node Content piece is a 'living' document, or 'content by committee'. In either case, it would be handy to have more than one version of the Node Content available—and you can, à la Revisions!

What you will learn
In this chapter, you will learn about:

- Enhancing layouts with HTML and CSS
- Creating a content include file
- Enabling a content include file with PHP
- Revising Node Content
- Managing Node Content revisions

What you will do

In this chapter, you will

- Create a CSS file, and instruct Drupal to use it with our theme
- Create a Page containing table data
- Add CSS formatting to the table data
- Create an include file
- Use a template in the new page via PHP
- Create a Revision

Enhancing layouts with HTML and CSS

We will be using HTML and CSS to style our next piece of Node Content. A thorough discussion of HTML and CSS is beyond the scope of this book, but let's have a short primer on the pieces that we will be using.

HTML and tables

You may have seen tables in web pages. They resemble the row and column structure of a spreadsheet. We're going to use the Rich Text Editor to create a table, but knowing the structure will make it easier for us to edit it, and to troubleshoot it (if necessary). The following table gives us an overview of the structure.

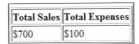

Total Sales	Total Expenses
$700	$100

A table in HTML is made up of a minimum of three types of tags. They are: table, row, and cell. Each table has one or more rows, and each row has one or more cells. So, a table, like the one we just saw, is structured as:

```
Table
      Row
            Cell
            Cell
      Row
            Cell
            Cell
```

This same table is created using HTML, as follows:

```
<table border="1">
    <tr>
        <th>Total Sales</th>
        <th>Total Expenses</th>
    </tr>
    <tr>
        <td>$700</td>
        <td>$100</td>
    </tr>
</table>
```

Let's look at what these tags are:

`<table>  </table>` Start and end tags to define a table; 1 pair per table

`<tr>  </tr>` Start and end tags to define a table row; 1 pair per row

`<th>  </th>` Start and end tags to define a heading cell; 1 pair per cell

`<td>  </td>` Start and end tags to define a data cell; 1 pair per cell

CSS in Drupal

CSS can be as complex and lengthy a subject as HTML. So we'll just take a look at the small subset that we'll use the most.

Just as HTML is used for creating tables, **CSS (Cascading Style Sheets)** styles are used to dress them up a bit, so that they don't look dull and boring like the previous example.

Every theme in Drupal comes with at least one CSS file, which is usually called `style.css`. This file contains styles that affect the appearance of the HTML elements within the page (such as headings, text, tables, and images). We could make changes to the file that comes with our theme, but if a new version were to be released, we'd have to make the changes again. Fortunately, there's an easier way. We can add one line of code to the file that describes the theme, and tells it to expect an extra CSS file. Then, having done that, we can create our own CSS file.

A theme is like a web site's wardrobe. With Drupal, a theme is a set of files, styles, and graphics that determine where the content will appear on the page, how it will look, including the typography, borders, navigation buttons, and colors. Sometimes, the visual part of a theme is also referred to as a 'skin'.

Activity 4.1: Adding a CSS file to a theme

In this activity, we'll learn how to incorporate custom CSS files into the theme of our choice.

We'll open the theme information file. This file is located in the directory `/themes` of our web site, and in the subdirectory matching our theme name. We're using the Analytic theme. Therefore, the file will be located in the `/sites/all/themes/analytic` directory, and will be called `analytic.info`.

1. The first few lines of the file look like this:

```
name = Analytic
description = Theme for ...provided by RussianWebStudio.com
core = 6.x
engine = phptemplate
```

These lines tell us the name of the theme, give us a brief description of it, and tell us which version of Drupal the theme is to be used with.

2. Just beneath the line `engine = phptemplate` we're going to add:

```
stylesheets[all][] = style.css
stylesheets[all][] = customization.css
```

Normally, the file `style.css` will automatically have a line added to the web page to link to it. However, because we are specifying a CSS file `customization.css`, we must also specify the `style.css` file, or it will not be linked, as Drupal not only allows us to add a CSS file, but also to replace the default CSS file. Therefore, we will list both the files to let Drupal know that we need both.

Activity 4.2: Creating a CSS file

Because we have already specified our custom CSS file in *Activity 4.1*, let's now code the file to our specific needs.

1. We need to create the CSS file itself. It's just a text file, and we only need to have a few lines in it:

```
tr.striped-odd {background-color: #fff4c0}
tr.striped-even {background-color: #ffffff}
```

Both of these lines define the appearance of a table row, depending on the count (even/odd) the table row refers to. We'll get to that shortly. They will be used to color the background of alternating table rows.

2. Let's add one more row to our CSS file:

```
table.striped {border: 1px solid #000000}
```

This line will create a border around our table that is more visually pleasing than the one in our earlier example.

3. We'll save the file as `customization.css` and put it in the same directory, `/themes/analytic`.

That's it! We've created a stylesheet. We'll add some more styles to it in the next activity, and we'll use the styles later in the chapter.

Activity 4.3: Creating an 'include' file

An 'include' file is a file that has content—HTML, CSS, and so on—and can be 'included' or imported into another file dynamically, instead of having all of the content within a single file. This makes it easier to segregate instructions by type, or functionality, or both, and also allows instructions to be reused, rather than having several copies of them in several files, with all of them needing to be modified whenever a change is needed.

> In fact, the content of an included file is no different than a normal file with the same content. Often, the file extension will be `.inc`, and it may be located in a directory called `/includes` (or something similar), but within the file, nothing special is needed. The 'include' is done by the file in which the content needs to be incorporated.

For this activity, we will be creating an include file that provides a footer for the content, as opposed to the footer for the entire web page. Then, we will add some styles to our stylesheet, which will provide formatting for this footer.

1. We'll create another text file.

2. In this text file, we'll add the following HTML:

```
<div id="ref-footer">
<span>This information is Copyright &copy;2008- Frank Bozak. All
Rights Reserved.</span>
</div>
```

> Using special characters in web pages can be problematic. Just because your Word Processor will insert a bullet or an accented character doesn't mean that it will be understood within HTML. Therefore, there are HTML codes for the most common characters that aren't on your keyboard. For instance, © produces the copyright symbol ©.

3. We'll do one more thing to this file. We're going to insert a PHP snippet (small piece of code), in order to provide some functionality that HTML cannot provide.

 PHP is a programming language, or more precisely, a scripting language, as its instructions do not need to be compiled in order to be used. Believe it or not, PHP stands for **PHP Hypertext Processor**, one of the few examples of an acronym being contained in its own acronym.

We specified '2008' above as the copyright, but that is actually the starting date (at the time of writing, the year is 2009). We could type '2008-2009', but then we'd have to remember to change the latter part next year. It would be great if we could have the second year change automatically, and we can, by using PHP. Between the hyphen and the space after it, we'll type:

```
<?php echo date('Y'); ?>
```

The line of code now looks like this:

```
...&copy;2008-<?php echo date('Y'); ?> Frank...
```

The opening and closing tags `<?php` and `?>` announce that what lies between them should be interpreted as PHP script and not as HTML. Let's take a quick look at the PHP statement. The `echo` command displays the message that follows it, on the web page. The `date()` command generates a date in the format specified (`'Y'` being a four-digit year). In this case, it will generate the four-digit year of the current date. The semicolon ends the statement. The result is that, if the page is looked at in 2011, it will show '©2008-2011'.

 PHP can also be used directly within Node Content, and entered into the Body text box. In order for it to be interpreted correctly, the PHP module needs to be enabled, and the **Input format** needs to be changed to **PHP code**, even though the body will most likely contain a blend of PHP, HTML, and text. The **Input format** link is below the Body text box. If PHP is not one of the choices, then the **PHP filter** module needs to be enabled. You can still save, and the PHP code will be there when you re-edit, but it will be disabled until the **PHP code** Input format is selected.

4. We'll save this file as `/ref-footer.inc`.

5. Now we need to add the styles to our stylesheet, as follows:

```
#ref-footer {
    background-image:url(images/bkimage.jpg) repeat;
    border: 1px solid #ccc;
```

```
    height: 40px
}
#ref-footer span {
    font-family: Tahoma, Arial, sans-serif;
    font-size: 10pt;
    font-weight: bold
    position: relative;
    top: 30%;
    margin-top: -24px
}
```

The first set of lines describes the boundary box of the footer, which will have a border and a background image (background images are good for filling boxes and allowing text to appear over them). The second set of lines describes the typeface that will be used for the text within the footer, and places a line in the vertical center of the footer.

At this point, we have created:

- A stylesheet that contains styles for the table and the footer
- An 'include' file containing the footer

What remains is to create the Node Content that uses these pieces. Because the structure of this Node Content is somewhat complex, it would be helpful to know what the plan is. Let's take a look at a wireframe diagram of the intended page, before we begin the activity.

Activity 4.4: Creating the Node Content header

The ultimate goal is to have three boxes at the top of the Node Content area, some text below that, then our table, and beneath the table, the footer. The three boxes can be created as a reusable include file (as we did with the footer). For now, we will consider them unique to the Node Content, and create them there.

1. Let's add one more style to our stylesheet. Even though we'll create the boxes within the body of our Node Content, having the particulars of the box in our stylesheet will lessen our typing.

   ```
   div.box-top {
       float: left;
       width: 32.5%;
       background-color: #e5efef;
       border: 1px solid #c1b4a3;
       border-collapse: collapse;
   }
   ```

2. Choose **Create content** from the admin menu, or add /node/add to the URL of the front page in your browser.

3. Select **Page** as the Node Content type.

4. We'll name the Page **Glossary**.

5. We're going to type the HTML directly into the Body text box, so let's click on the link below it to turn off the editor.

6. In the Body text box, we'll start with the HTML necessary for the three boxes. Let's take it a step at a time. First, the tags needed to create the three boxes, without content.

   ```
   <div>
   <div class="box-top"></div>
   <div class="box-top"></div>
   <div class="box-top"></div>
   <div style="clear: both;"></div>
   </div>
   ```

   A <div> is essentially a container. Notice that the closing tag for the first div doesn't occur until the end of the snippet. This means that it is a container for the other four div sets. Three of them define their class as 'box-top' (one of the styles that we created earlier). They will each be one of our boxes. Normally, a div will be positioned under the prior one. Our div sets will appear side-by-side, because we declared them in their style as float. The final div in the snippet has a style of clear: both. This is an instruction to end the floating, or else subsequent elements in our HTML could end up being arranged incorrectly.

7. Now, we'll turn on the editor for a moment, and we can see the three empty boxes, as shown in following screenshot.

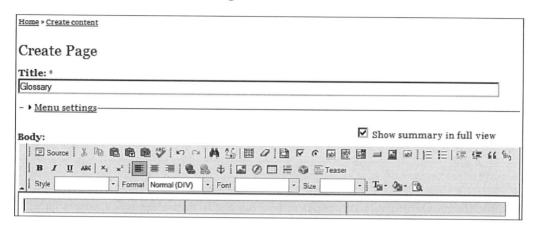

Sometimes the display doesn't update correctly when switching back and forth with the Rich Text Editor. If you only see two boxes, then try turning it off and then on again.

8. While the editor is active, we'll add content to each of the three boxes. The first box is going to contain an image, so we'll click on the **Insert/Edit Image** button, as shown in the screenshot below.

9. The Image editor dialog box will appear, and we'll click on the **Browse Server** button.

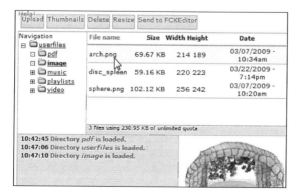

10. We'll select the file **arch.png**, and click on the **Send to FCKEditor** option to return to the Image editor.

11. Back in the Image editor, we'll add some **Alternate Text** (never miss an opportunity to use alternate text as fodder for the search engines), and click on the **OK** button.

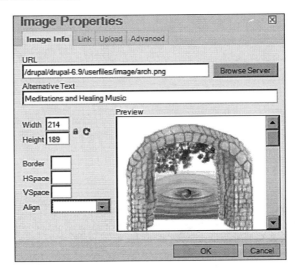

12. Click once inside the third box. We'll add a graphic here, too. Follow steps 9 to 11 again, but this time we'll select **sphere.png** as the image (shown in the following screenshot), and set the **Height** to **185**, as the original height of the image is too large.

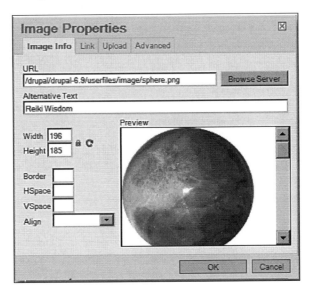

13. In the center box, we're going to have a quote. First, we'll turn off the editor and modify the `<div>` tag to add some styling. We could use the editor, but it's often easier to directly modify a tag. Immediately before the closing '>' in the tag, we'll add:

```
style="font-family: cursive; padding: 4px; font-size: 16pt;
height: 181px;"
```

14. With that in place, we can add the quote:

    In everyday life, harmony is generally accepted as living without tension. In music, harmony is the art of balancing tension.

15. If we turn on the editor now, then we'll see the three boxes with content. Let's select the quote with our mouse, and then click on the **Center Justify** text button.

16. With the text centered, the three boxes, which make up the header of our Node Content, are complete, and can be seen in the screenshot below.

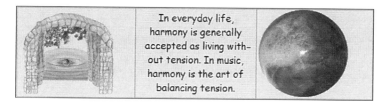

Activity 4.5: Creating the Node Content Body

We've put the header of our Node Content into place in the prior activity. Now we'll create the body of the Node Content, while taking advantage of the styles that we have created for our table in *Activity 4.1*.

We'll be able to do most of the work using the Rich Text Editor, and then fine-tune the appearance directly in the tags.

Hopefully, you're starting to realize that the Rich Text Editor cannot be used for everything. It's very convenient for minor formatting, but for formatting that requires finer granularity, it's usually easier to work directly with HTML.

1. We'll click in the Body text box, just below the three-box header, to begin a new paragraph, and type the following text:

Following are some of the 'technical' terms that you might come across on this site, and their respective meaning in the context of healing, music, Reiki and meditation.

We now have the text that we want, as seen in the following screenshot, but not in the format that we want. The text is too small, and in the wrong typeface.

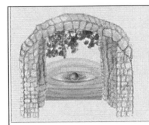
In everyday life, harmony is generally accepted as living with-out tension. In music, harmony is the art of balancing tension.

Following are some of the 'technical' terms that you might come across on this site, and their respective meaning in the context of healing, music, Reiki and meditation.

 Although a serif typeface such as Times New Roman is the easiest for reading body text on printed matter such as letters and newspapers, on the screen a sans-serif typeface, such as Tahoma, Arial, and Helvetica, is best.

2. We're using the FCKeditor, and it has two drop-down boxes for us to use. They are **Font** and **Format**. Let's select the text that we just entered, and then from the **Font** drop-down, we'll select **Tahoma** as the typeface.

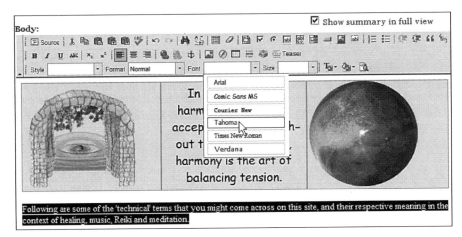

3. Now that we have the correct typeface, let's make the text bigger. With the text still selected, let's change the size to something less microscopic, by using the **Format** drop-down to select a predefined heading format: **Heading 3**.

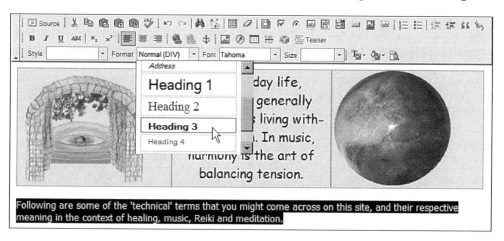

The altered text has an appearance that draws the eye more than the original text.

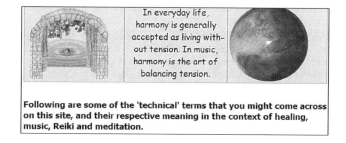

4. On to the important stuff. We need to create the table that will hold our glossary, and we can partly use the editor for this. First, we click below the heading text, and press *Enter* to create a new paragraph.

5. Then, we click on the **Insert/Edit Table** button to open the **Table Properties** dialog box.

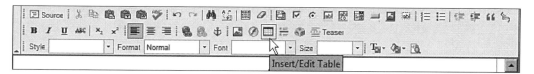

6. In the **Table Properties** editor, we'll change a few of the default settings:

Rows = 7

Alignment = Left

Width = 100 percent

The completed dialog is shown in the following screenshot. We will then click on the **OK** button.

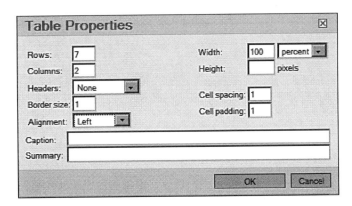

7. Now we have a skeleton table, as shown in screenshot below.

Following are some of the 'technical' terms that you might come across on this site, and their respective meaning in the context of healing, music, Reiki and meditation.	

Steps 2 to 4 are going to take advantage of an advanced formatting technique that is not something that Content Editors themselves would be called on to do. You can choose to ignore these steps, which will have the content differ only in the fact that each of the rows created, starting from Step 5, will have the same white background color, or you can choose to grit your teeth, scratch your head, and boldly go where no Content Editor has gone before!

8. It's at this point that we'll make use of CSS *and* PHP. We need to insert a Class selector in each row of the table, so that it will use the associated style. There is one class for odd-numbered rows and one class for even. We could apply them as such, but then we face a problem. If we ever insert a new row between the others, then the odd/even designation for the rest would be incorrect. Instead, we are going to put the same code in every table row tag, and this code will decide whether the row is odd or even, and request the appropriate class. Turn off the editor, or use the **Source** button to edit the tags.

9. Between the `<tbody>` tag and the first `<tr>` tag, insert the following:

```
<?php $rowctr=0;?>
```

This line sets our row counter to `0`.

10. Inside each opening `<tr>` tag, put a space between 'tr' and '>', and then insert the following snippet:

```
class="<?php echo ((++$rowctr)%2!=0)?"striped-odd":"striped-
even"?>"
```

This snippet adds 1 to the row counter, and then divides it by 2. If the remainder is `0`, it requests `class="striped-even"`, otherwise it requests `class="striped-odd"`.

 It's likely that the row formatting will not be visible until the page is saved.

Now we can add the terms and definitions to the table. The seven pairs are as shown in the following screenshot of the table. We can type the values directly into the table.

Aroma Therapy:	Inhaling and applying of essential plant or other oils intended to bring inner peace and well balance.
Akashic Records:	Fourth dimensional repository of thoughts, events and actions from the beginning of time.
Alternative Medicine:	Used in addition or in place of traditional medicine.
Attunement:	Balancing and integrating all of a body's energy systems.
Aura:	Energetic electromagnetic representation of a living form of energy.
Grounding:	Anchoring the root chakra to Mother Earth
Karma:	Universal Law of cause and effect

11. Next, we'll add our footer. We can do this by adding the following PHP snippet to the bottom of our `<body>`:

```php
<?php include('ref-footer.inc');
```

12. Finally, we'll create a menu link for this page, using the settings that are shown in the following screenshot.

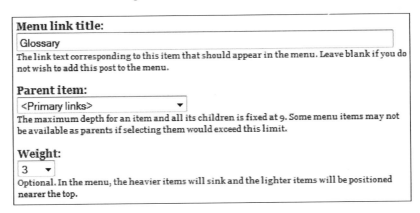

13. Remember, because we have used PHP in our Node Content, we need to click on the **Input format** link, and then select **PHP code** as our input type.

> The **PHP code** input type is usually not configured to make use of a Rich Text Editor, as the Rich Text Editor will not recognize the PHP code, and will strip it out. Therefore, when you click on **PHP code** for the input type, if the Rich Text Editor is open, the code will disappear.

14. The completed page is shown in the following screenshot.

Page *Glossary* has been created.

Home

Glossary

View | Edit

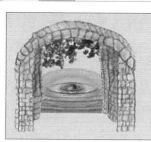

In everyday life, harmony is generally accepted as living without tension. In music, harmony is the art of balancing tension.

Following are some of the 'technical' terms that you might come across on this site, and their respective meaning in the context of healing, music, Reiki and meditation.

Aroma Therapy:	Inhaling and applying of essential plant or other oils intended to bring inner peace and well balance.
Akashic Records:	Fourth dimensional repository of thoughts, events and actions from the beginning of time.
Alternative Medicine:	Used in addition or in place of traditional medicine.
Attunement:	Balancing and integrating all of a body's energy systems.
Aura:	Energetic electromagnetic representation of a living form of energy.
Grounding:	Anchoring the root chakra to Mother Earth
Karma:	Universal Law of cause and effect

You won't find any PHP code in the HTML of the web page shown by your browser. PHP code is evaluated by the server, on which the web site resides, and the resulting output of the PHP is what appears in the web page. PHP privileges should not be given to normal users, because havoc can be wreaked upon the web site, intentionally or not, through the use of PHP.

Revisions

We've created our glossary in the previous activities. So, the question arises, what if we need to add glossary terms? Of course, we can edit the Page, and add the terms to it, just as we can edit any Node Content.

There is one thing to keep in mind with regards to editing Node Content. Once you have changed it, and saved it, the original contents are gone. If you change your mind, then you're in a bad position. Unless, that is, you create a revision, instead of simply editing the content.

A revision is another version of the same page, but instead of existing as separate pages, there is one page with revision versions.

 Node Content types can be edited (admin/content/types), and the settings changed to make Revisions the default option. In this case, the **Create new revision** checkbox will be selected by default.

We'll finish this chapter by making a revision to our glossary, and learn how to work with revisions, in the process.

Activity 4.6: Creating a Revision

We're going to make a few simple changes to our **Glossary** page, and save the changed page as a revision of the original.

1. We'll click on the **Edit** tab of the **Glossary** Page, and turn on the Rich Text Editor, if it is not already showing.

2. We're going to do two things to each term in the left column:
    ○ Remove the colon following the term
    ○ Select the text and make it bold

    The table with the changes incorporated into it is shown in following screenshot.

Aroma Therapy	Inhaling and applying of essential plant or other oils intended to bring inner peace and well balance.
Akashic Records	Fourth dimensional repository of thoughts, events and actions from the beginning of time.
Alternative Medicine	Used in addition or in place of traditional medicine.
Attunement	Balancing and integrating all of a body's energy systems.
Aura	Energetic electromagnetic representation of a living form of energy.
Grounding	Anchoring the root chakra to Mother Earth
Karma	Universal Law of cause and effect

3. Next, down towards the bottom of the page, you will find the heading **Revision information**. We'll click on it to open the dialog, and complete the revision information as follows:

   ○ We'll select the checkbox labeled **Create new revision**.

   ○ We'll add two lines to the **Log message** text box: **Removed the colons following each term Made each term bold**.

4. We'll click on the **Save** button, and we now have a revision of our Page.

You will see that in addition to the normal tabs of **View** and **Edit**, there is now a tab labeled **Revisions**. Let's click on that tab. The **Revision** page (shown in the upcoming screenshot) lists the original version of the Page and each revision, along with the creation date and time. Under the **Operations** heading, the **current revision** is also labeled, but the earlier revisions offer the option of reverting to them, or deleting them. The notes that we entered in the **Log message** text box are shown. This makes it easier to determine what the changes accompanied with each revision are.

If you commonly use Revisions on your site, then an add-on module that will greatly benefit you is **Diff**, which can be found at `http://drupal.org/project/diff`. This module provides a tab that shows the revisions for a Node Content item, as well as the differences in each revision.

The date and time of each revision is in itself a link. To view a revision, other than the current version, simply click on that link. Of course, you cannot edit a revision, other than the current one, unless you revert to that version first.

Home » Glossary

The revisions let you track differences between multiple versions of a post.

Revisions for *Glossary*

View	Edit	**Revisions**	
Revision			**Operations**
03/08/2009 - 11:02pm by admin Removed the colons following each term Made each term bold			*current revision*
03/08/2009 - 10:33pm by admin			revert delete

Summary

In this chapter we learned about:

- Enhancing layouts with HTML and CSS
- Creating a content include file
- Enabling a content include file with PHP
- Revising Node Content
- Managing Node Content revisions

These topics were explained with the help of activities where we:

- Created a CSS file and instructed Drupal to use it with our theme
- Created a Page that contained table data
- Added CSS formatting to the table data
- Created an include file
- Used a template in the new page via PHP
- Created a Revision

In Chapter 5, we will learn about making our Node Content easier to find.

5
Making Content Findable

We've created some Node Content in the last three chapters. Interesting and useful content is a necessity on any web site, particularly on those built around a Content Management System. However, this may not be the only necessity. Another necessity is making the browsing experience on your site pleasant for the visitor, and in this context, making the content easy to find. Having content on the front page of the site is one way to make it findable, but the amount of content is limited to a point before the page becomes unwieldy. In this chapter, we will make it easier for site visitors to find our content in a number of ways.

What you will learn

In this chapter, you will learn about:

- Using Taxonomy to link descriptive terms to Node Content
- Tag clouds
- Path aliases

What you will do

In this chapter, you will:

- Create a Taxonomy
- Enable the use of tags with Node Content
- Define a custom URL
- Activate site searching
- Perform a search

Understanding Taxonomy

One way to find content on a site is by using a search function, but this can be considered as a hit-or-miss approach. Searching for an article on 'canines' won't return an article about dogs, unless it contains the word 'canines'.

Certainly, navigation provides a way to navigate the site, but unless your site has only a small amount of content, the navigation can only be general in nature. Too much navigation is annoying. There are far too many sites with two or three sets of top navigation, plus left and bottom navigation. It's just too much to take in and still feel relaxed.

Site maps offer additional navigation assistance, but they're usually not fun to read, and are more like a Table of Contents, where you have to know what you're looking for.

So, what's the answer? — Tags!

A **Tag** is simply a word or a phrase that is used as a descriptive link to content. In Drupal, a collective set of terms, from which terms or tags are associated with content, is called a **Vocabulary**. One or more Vocabularies comprise a Taxonomy. This a good place to begin, so let's create a Vocabulary.

Activity 5.1: Creating a Taxonomy Vocabulary

In this activity, we will be adding two terms to our Vocabulary. We shall also learn how to assign a Taxonomy to Node Content that has been created.

1. We begin in the **Content management** area of the **admin** menu. There, you should find the **Taxonomy** option listed, as shown in the following screenshot. Click on this option.

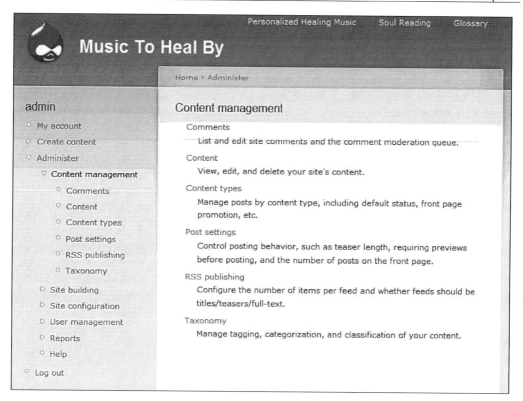

Taxonomy isn't listed in my admin menu

The **Taxonomy** module is not enabled by default. Check on the **Modules** page (**Admin | Site building | Modules**) and make sure that the module is enabled.

For the most part, modules can be thought of as options that can be added to your Drupal site, although some of them are considered essential. Some modules come pre-installed with Drupal. Among them, some are automatically activated, and some need to be activated manually. There are many modules that are not included with Drupal, but are available freely from the Drupal web site. The process of obtaining and installing modules is beyond the scope of this book, but the URL where they can be found is given in *Appendix B*.

2. The next page gives us a lengthy description of the use of a taxonomy. At the top of the page are two options, **List** and **Add vocabulary**. We'll choose the latter.

3. On the **Add vocabulary** page, we need to provide a **Vocabulary name**. We can create several vocabularies, each for a different use. For example, with this site, we could have a vocabulary for 'Music' and another for 'Meditation'. For now, we'll just create one vocabulary, and name it **Tags**, as suggested below, in the **Vocabulary name** box.

4. In the **Description** box, we'll type **This vocabulary contains Tag terms**.

5. In the **Help text** box, we'll type **Enter one or more descriptive terms separated by commas**.

6. Next is the [Node] **Content types** section. This lists the types of Node Content that are currently defined. Each has a checkbox alongside it. Selecting the checkbox indicates that the associated Node Content type can have Tags from this vocabulary assigned to it. Ultimately, it means that if a site visitor searches using a Tag, then this type of Node Content might be offered as a match. We will be selecting all of the checkboxes.

 If a new Node Content type is created that will use tags, then edit the vocabulary and select the checkbox.

7. The **Settings** section defines how we will use this vocabulary. In this case, we want to use it with tags, so we will select the **Tags** checkbox.

8. The following screenshot shows the completed page. We'll then click on the **Save** button.

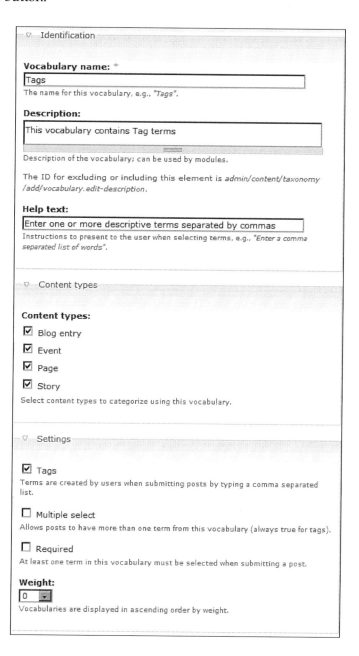

9. At this point, we have a vocabulary, as shown in the screenshot, but it doesn't contain anything. We need to add *something* to it, so that we can use it. Let's click on the **add terms** link.

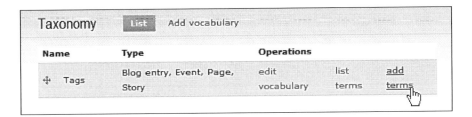

10. On the **Add term** page, we're going to add two terms, one at a time. First we'll type **healing music** into the **Term name** box. We'll purposely make the terms lower case, as it will look better in the display that we'll be creating soon.

11. We'll click on the **Save** button, and then repeat the procedure for another term named **meditation**.

12. The method we used for adding terms is acceptable when creating new terms that have not been applied to anything, yet. If the term does apply to existing Node Content, then a better way to add it is by editing that content. We'll edit the Page we created, entitled **Soul Reading**. Now that the site has the **Taxonomy** module enabled, a new field named **Tags** appears below **Title**. We're going to type **soul reading** into it. This is an AJAX field. If we start typing a tag that already exists, then it will offer to complete the term.

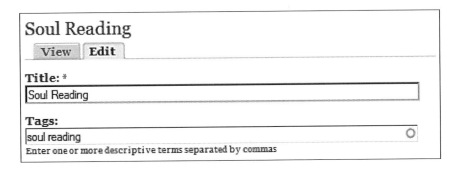

 AJAX (Asynchronous JavaScript + XML) is a method of using existing technologies to retrieve data in the background. What it means to a web site visitor is that data can be retrieved and presented on the page being viewed, without having to reload the page.

13. Now, we can **Save** our Node Content, and return to the vocabulary that we created earlier. Click on the **List** tab at the top of the page. Our terms are listed, as shown in the following screenshot.

Terms in *Tags*	List	Add term	
Name		**Operations**	
healing music		edit	
meditation		edit	
soul reading		edit	

Tag Clouds

In computer terminology, a **Cloud** is a gathering of loosely-related items with something in common. An example of such a phenomenon is a playground at a fast-food restaurant where several highways intersect. The kids aren't necessarily tied by ethnicity, nationality, age, sex, citizenship, home town, destination, nor 'herd'. The two commonalities are that they're all kids and all Homo Sapiens (although, they might seem like they are from Alpha Centauri).

A **Tag Cloud** is a grouping of terms that don't necessarily have any relationship to each other with regards to their meaning or context. The only factor that typically links the terms is that they are all related to the content on the same web site.

Tag Clouds are normally represented as a rectangular region in which the terms appear as different typefaces and font-sizes, so that each term stands out from its neighbor. We're going to use two types of Drupal Tag Clouds, which means that two different modules will be used in order to show us different examples. The first one is called Tagadelic, and the other, Cumulus. The only difference between the two is that Cumulus presents the tags as a flash movie. Putting one's mouse over the cloud causes the tags to start moving within the cloud as if it were in 3D and they were hailstones. The words actually appear to move away (get smaller) and cycle around as they draw closer again.

The **Cumulus** module depends on the presence of the **Tagadelic** module, both are add-on modules. Even though both are present, the **Tagadelic** module's output doesn't need to be enabled on the page, unless you want it to be shown. We're going to use one of each Cloud type. Each Tag Cloud module creates a **Block** for its Tag Cloud. We'll be taking a look at Blocks in the next chapter. For now, both modules have been configured and assigned to the right-hand column. These modules, as well as the tags, can be seen in the following screenshot.

We named the Tagadelic tag cloud, **Index**, and the Cumulus tag cloud as **Cumulus Tag Cloud**. Both of them present the tags as links. We'll click on the link for **meditation**, and the result is shown in the following screenshot.

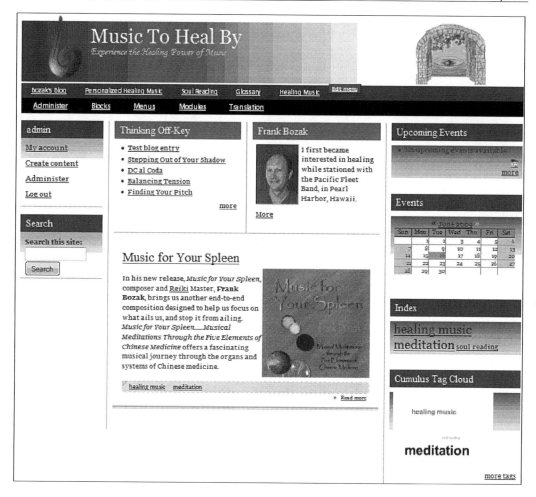

My Tags Don't Show Up

When new Tags are added, there are two things that you may need to do in order for them to appear in the tag cloud. The configuration for the Cumulus tag cloud has a **Clear Cache** button, and the **Performance** page (admin/settings/performance) has one as well. They are two different caches. Moreover, even though the **Performance** page might say that caching is disabled, theme contents are still cached, so click on the cache-clearing buttons at both locations.

The whole idea of the Tag Clouds is that a site visitor, without knowing much, or knowing little-to-nothing about your site's content, can scan the tags for a subject that they are interested in, and click on it.

Path Aliases

Every web page that you visit has an address, or URL, that is listed in the address bar of your web browser. If you've paid attention to the URLs in your web browser, then you've probably seen quite a few that look as though they span a paragraph in length. This doesn't affect the visitor's ability to get to the page. After all, clicking on a link is clicking a link, regardless of its size. However, if the person tries to remember the link, or needs to write it down, then it gets ugly. Beyond that, it's nice to have URLs that are actually meaningful for the search engine 'spiders' that crawl the Web and index everything.

This begs the question, "where do the URLs come from?" The answer, with regards to Drupal, is that they are created by the software, and they're not pretty. Here is the URL for the *Soul Reading* page that we just looked at.

http://mydomain.com/node/15

Not very helpful at all, is it? Fortunately, we can make this link much nicer to look at, and much more meaningful. Drupal comes with a **Path** module. The term 'path' refers to the portion of the URL that follows the domain name: **node/15** in the example above. The **Path** module allows us to create an alias path. The original path will still exist and be usable (Drupal will continue to use it internally), but the path that is presented to the site visitor (and the search engines) will be the alias. Let's create an alias for one of our articles.

Activity 5.2: Creating a Path Alias

We'll edit *Music for Your Spleen*. Beneath the **Comment settings** link is a link to the **URL path settings** option. If it's not present, then the **Path** module needs to be installed and/or enabled. Click on the link to open the dialog.

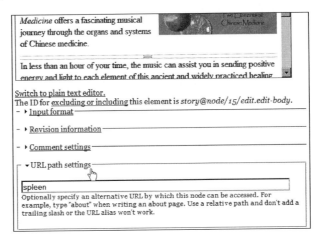

In the text box provided, we'll simply enter **spleen**, and then **Save** the Story.

Now, the URL for the page is as seen in the address bar of the browser in the following screenshot.

Searching

Aside from the navigational aids, one of the landmarks that site visitors always expect to see is the search box. It's very frustrating when a site's navigation doesn't offer a path to where you want to go, and there's no search box to be found.

Activity 5.3: Enabling the Search functionality

The **Search** module is included with Drupal. All that we need to do is to turn it on, and tell Drupal where we want it to appear.

1. We'll select the **Site Building** option from the **Administer** menu, and in the **Site Building** option, we'll select the **Modules** option.

2. Some way down the page is the heading named **Core**. The modules listed in this section are part of the Drupal installation. We select the checkbox next to **Search**, and then click on the **Save Configuration** button at the bottom of the page.

3. Next, we'll click on the **Blocks** option from the **Administer** menu.

4. On the **Blocks** page, towards the bottom of the **Disabled** section, we find a row for the **Search form** option. Beside the name, we'll click on the arrow in the drop-down list box, and then select the **left sidebar** option, as shown in the screenshot below.

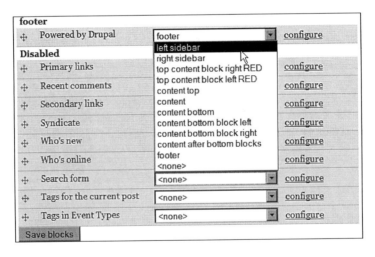

5. The row has now moved higher up the page to the **left sidebar** section. We need to click on the **Save blocks** button at the bottom of the screen to save our change.

6. Next, return to the **Home** page, which is the front page, and we find the **Search** box in the left column. We'll enter **healing** into the box, as shown in the following screenshot.

7. The **Search results** are shown in the screenshot that follows. You'll also notice that at the top of the results is a link for an **Advanced search**, should the search need to be made more granular.

 Searching and advanced searching are actions that are controlled by permissions, so the search box and/or the advanced search link may not be visible to every user role.

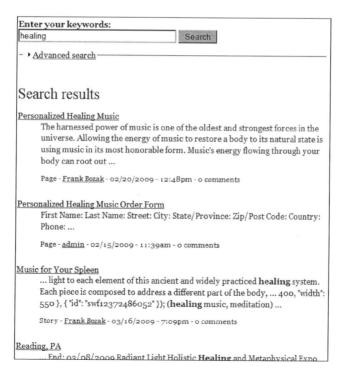

My searches yield no results

If your searches consistently return no results, then it is because the site has not been indexed. Navigating to the **Reports** menu from the **Administer** menu, and then to the **Status Report**, will lead you to a link for running Cron manually. This will cause the site to be indexed.

Summary

In this chapter we learned about:

- Using Taxonomy to link descriptive terms to Node Content
- Tag clouds
- Path Aliases

These topics have been learnt with the help of activities in which we:

- Created a taxonomy
- Enabled the use of tags with Node Content
- Defined a custom URL
- Enabled site searching
- Performed a search

In Chapter 6, we will learn about exciting Rich Content types!

6
Rich Content Types

Looking back at what we have learned so far, we can have an article as a Page on our web page, or a few articles (or article teasers) as Stories. These two types of Node Content will probably represent the bulk of the content on most sites, but there are additional, richer forms of content that we can spruce up our site with, and that's just what we're going to do!

What you will learn

In this chapter, we will learn how to enhance our Drupal site using:

- **Blocks**—the tiny building blocks of a content-rich site
- **Views**—the grouping of Stories of similar content on one page
- **Blogs**—a Web-based interactive diary

What you will do

In this chapter, you will be:

- Creating a Block as an advertisement that appears outside of the normal Node Content area
- Creating a View to display the selected Node Content, based on taxonomy vocabulary terms
- Creating a blog entry, and then commenting on it

The good side of being a Blockhead

What if we want an advertisement, or other such content of the same size? We could use HTML to add it to a Page or Story. However, what if we want them to appear in many Stories without making a copy in each one, or if we want them to appear outside of the Story's margins, such as on the side of the web page? What if we want the advertisement or other content to be independent of the Page or the Story? The answer to these questions is: Blocks. Let's create a Block to advertise a CD. We already have an article about the CD, but this Block will be used where the article cannot.

Activity 6.1: Creating a Block

Let's take a step-by-step approach to create a Block to advertise the CD.

1. Log in as the admin, and then select the **Site building** menu.

2. The **Site building** menu will be similar to the following screenshot (it may vary based on the installed modules). Next, we click on the **Blocks** option.

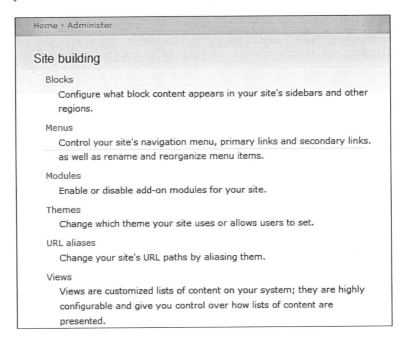

3. The **Blocks** page looks somewhat different from other admin pages. Its layout is discussed in the section *Deciphering the Blocks page*. Below the page name are two tabs, as seen in the following screenshot. Click on the **Add block** tab.

4. The first field on the Create block form(**Block description**) is a required field. This entry will be listed as the description for the block being created on the Blocks page. We'll call this Block **Ad-Spleen**.

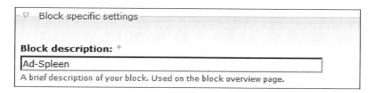

5. The **Block title** field is used to enter the display title. We're not going to have a title on the web page. Therefore, we'll let the content of the Block speak for itself.

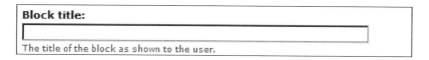

6. The **Block body** field will contain the meat of our content, just like the Body field for a Page or Story. We'll start by putting a 'wrapper' around our block, by enclosing it between a pair of tags. In this way, we can later define some CSS attributes (such as background color and width) for the HTML tags, which will then apply to everything inside the tags. The HTML tag that can be used as such a wrapper is called a 'div', the short form for division. It comes in a pair of `<div>` `</div>` tags that will be used at the beginning and the end of what it will wrap. Click on the **Create Div Container** button, as shown in the following screenshot.

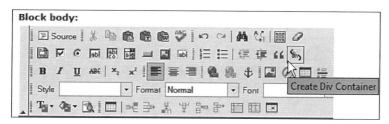

7. In the **Create Div Container** pop-up, we'll click on the **Advanced** tab. In the **Inline Style** text box, we'll add some CSS rules to the div tag (as shown in the upcoming screenshot), and then click on the **OK** button. The three styles entered in the text box do the following:

   ○ Width—sets the width of the div, which we've set to the width of the right-hand sidebar, because that's where we'll have the div

   ○ text-align—specifies that all of the text within the div will be centered, unless overridden

   ○ background-color—sets the inside color of the div, for which we have defined a light gold (#c0c000)

 Upon creating the div, a colored stripe will be the only clue, but it's there!

   ○ The first piece of content that we'll add to our Block will be an image. Let's click on the **Insert/Edit Image** button.

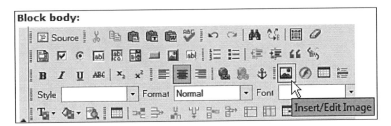

○ In the **Image Properties** popup, we'll click on the **Browse Server** button. Next, in the file browser, we'll select the image **disc_spleen.png**, and then click on the **Send to FCKEditor** button.

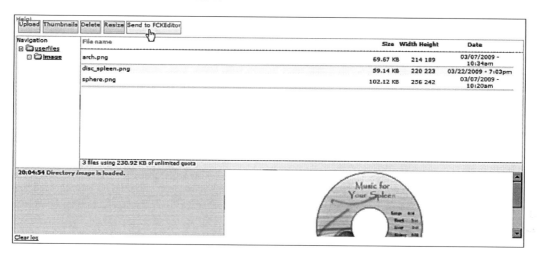

○ The image URL and dimensions, as well as an image preview, will appear in the **Image Properties** pop-up, as shown in the following screenshot. We'll add information to some of the other fields as follows:

Alternative Text: **Music for Your Spleen-Healing Music-Frank Bozak**

Border: 0

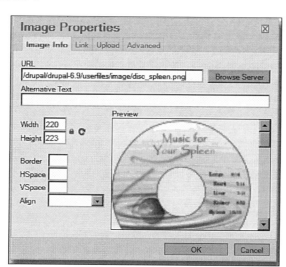

8. Next, we'll click on the **Link** tab. Depending on the Rich Text Editor that you use, and the options that have been installed on it, you may have the ability to link directly to Node Content by navigating to it from this window. Normally, a relative URL (just the portion that needs to be added to the page location in order to find the image) would be used. However, at the time of writing this book, the image browser did not work with relative URLs. Therefore, the complete URL has to be entered, as shown in the following screenshot.

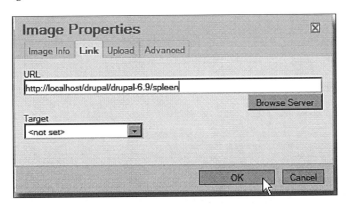

9. Back in the **Block body** editor window, we'll add some text. We want the text to appear below the image, as seen in the upcoming screenshot. The text to be entered is:

    Click to read more about this Healing Music CD

I can't get the text in the right place

If you can't seem to find a place to put the cursor (where the text appears) beneath the image with the gold color behind it, then you can use the **Source** button, or turn off the editor. You can then insert the text immediately before the closing div tag </div>.

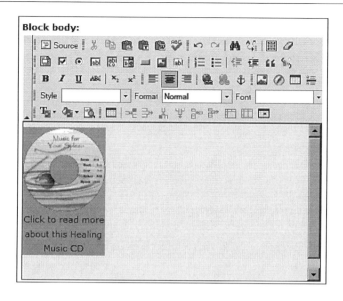

10. With our text entered, we'll select it by using the mouse, and then click on the **Bold** button (shown in the following screenshot). This will make the text stand out.

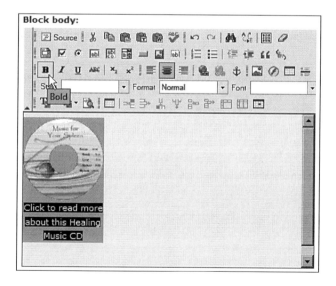

11. We've finished creating our Block content. Now, we need to configure the Block itself. Below the **Block body** box, we will click on the **Input format** link to expand the field set, and then select the **Full HTML** option, as shown in the following screenshot.

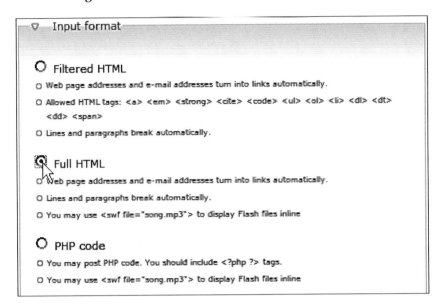

I put an image in my Block, but I can't see it on the page

If your block is visible on the web page (outside of the admin Block page), but some of its elements are not, then you may have forgotten to select the **Full HTML** option as your **Input format** (instead of the default Filtered HTML option). Edit the Block, and change this setting.

12. The next field set on the Blocks page is the **User specific visibility settings**. We're going to set it so that the block will always be seen.

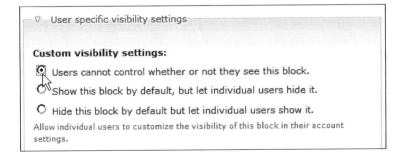

13. The **Page specific visibility settings** fieldset is where we can specify on which page(s) we want the Block to appear. The default setting would be for the Block to appear on every page. However, we don't want the Block to appear when someone is reading the full *Music for Your Spleen* article, as they're already on the page that the Block link would take them to. We'll choose to have the Block appear on every page *except* the one(s) we list. So, we'll enter **spleen** here (as seen in the screenshot), because that's the custom path name that we gave to that Node Content; that is, the page is reached via `mydomain.com/spleen`.

14. At this point, we can save the Block, after which we'll be returned to the Blocks list. At first, it might seem as though our Block hasn't been saved, as it doesn't seem to be in the list. The Block list appears in the order of the selectable regions on the page, starting from the upper-left. Our block hasn't been assigned to a region yet, so we need to scroll down to the **Disabled** section at the end of the list, and we will find it there.

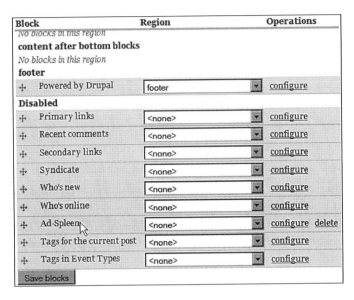

15. Because we know where we want to place the block, we'll assign the region to it. Click on the drop-down list box, and select the **right sidebar** option.

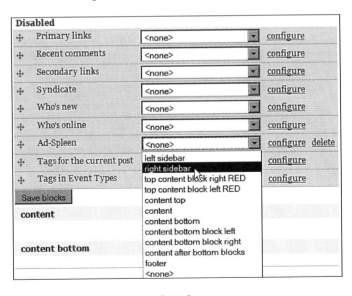

16. Having selected the region, our Block entry disappears from the **Disabled** section. It's moved up the list into the **right sidebar** section. By the way, we could have moved it there by dragging and dropping the Block entry. What I want to point out, though, is the message that you will now see above the **Save blocks** button. Your Block was saved, but the change to its region that you just made has not yet been saved. If you navigate away from this page without clicking on the **Save blocks** button, then the position will not be saved. Let's click on the button now.

> * The changes to these blocks will not be saved until the *Save blocks* button is clicked.
>
> Save blocks

17. The only thing left to do is to visit the front page, and see our new block. If we click on the image in it, then we're taken to the article about the CD. We can also see that the Block is not on this page, because we specified in its settings that it should not be.

Deciphering the Blocks page

The Blocks page might look a little daunting at first, but the layout is very useful, once you're acquainted with it. The page combines elements such as:

- A listing of the Blocks defined for the site
- A button for each of the themes that are enabled
- A segregation of the Blocks based on the region they are assigned to, for the theme with the selected button
- A label to show where each region is located on the page

Each block can be assigned to a region specific to a theme, so that, for example, it can be assigned to the right-hand sidebar in one theme, and the left-hand sidebar in another. However, a block *cannot* be assigned to different positions within the same theme. For example, if we wanted our Block to appear in a different location on the front page than on other pages, we would have to create another block altogether. There is a module available (called Multiblock, found at `drupal.org/project/multiblock`) that provides the capability to have more than one instance of a block. That would be the way to go.

Determining the Block widths

Sometimes a Block has no bounding box, nor background, as ours does. In this case, there really isn't a need to know how wide to make it, as the text will simply flow within the bounds of the region to which the Block is assigned. However, when using images, or bounding boxes, we will want the Block to be no larger than the region, and usually it should be as close to the size of the region as possible, in order to make efficient use of the space.

So, how do we know how wide the region is? The easiest way is to measure it—the way I do it is to make a copy of the screen, and paste it into a photo editing or drawing application. Then I select a rectangle the full width of the region using a crop tool, and look at the status bar to see how large a selection I have. The following screenshot shows the area of the selection, with a lasso around the image size in the status bar.

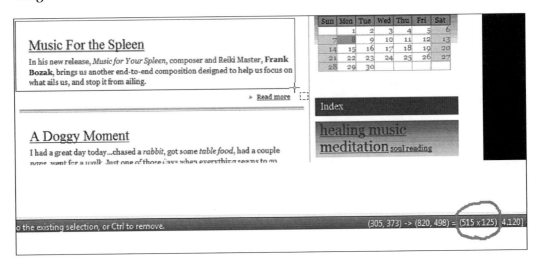

Taking a copy of the screen is the only tricky part, if you don't know how to do it. On a Windows machine, you could simply use the *Prt Scr* (Print Screen) key. This key copies the current display to the clipboard, then you simply paste it into whichever application you want to use. On a Mac, you can use the *Command+Shift+3* key combination to capture the entire screen, or the *Command+Shift+4* key combination to use cross-hairs to capture just the portion of the screen that you want. In Linux, you'll want to use the **Gimp** utility, which can also be used to edit the captured screen to determine the size of the region.

Views

As you have seen, a Vocabulary allows you to assign descriptive tags to the content. You may also have noticed that only the front page shows multiple pieces of Node Content, that there is only single front page, and that the criteria for Node Content appearing on this front page is simply whether that Node Content has been promoted or not.

So, it would seem that we have a disconnect. For example, what if we want a page to contain some or all (but more than one) of our pieces about healing music? It would seem that there's no way to do that. But there is—Views.

A View is basically a page based on the criteria that you specify. Thus, if your criteria is that you want it to show all of the Node Content with a Taxonomy value of *Healing Music*, then you will have accomplished the seemingly impossible. Let's do just that!

Activity 6.2: Creating a View

We're going to create a View to show articles on the topic of *Healing Music*. This will be like a front page for a particular category of Node Content.

1. From the admin menu, select the **Site building** option.
2. On the **Site building** menu, we'll select the **Views** option.
3. The Views page begins in **List** mode, and will have several Views that are predefined. There are four mode choices at the top of the page, as shown in the following screenshot. We'll click on the **Add** button.

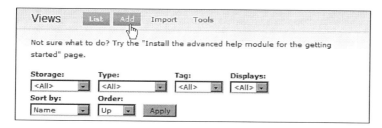

4. We are now on the first page of the View add process. Even though a View will typically be showing Node Content, the creation of Views is different from the creation of Node Content in several ways, but one way in particular. When we click on the **Next** button at the bottom of this page, the View still exists, even though we're not finished defining it. The information on this page cannot be changed once we move on. There is a mention to this effect, made above the **Next** button. The first field on this page is the **View name**. We'll call our view **Healing_Music**.

> **View name:** *
> Healing_Music

5. The next field is used for a description that will be shown in the View list. It's for our benefit and not for the site visitor, so we'll just type a little description to remind us of what the View is for.

> **View description:**
> content about healing music

6. We'll bypass the View tag field, and go to the **View type** fieldset. This is an important fieldset, as it defines the type of View that we will be creating, and once saved, cannot be changed. Our View will be using Node Content as the source material, so we will select **Node** as the type, and then click on the **Next** Button.

> **View type:**
>
> ⦿ Node
> Nodes are a Drupal site's primary content.
>
> ○ Comment
> Comments are responses to node content.
>
> ○ File
> Files maintained by Drupal and various modules.
>
> ○ Node revision
> Node revisions are a history of changes to nodes.
>
> ○ Term
> Taxonomy terms are attached to nodes.
>
> ○ User
> Users who have created accounts on your site.
>
> The view type is the primary table for which information is being retrieved. The view type controls what arguments, fields, sort criteria and filters are available, so once this is set it **cannot be changed**.

7. And wow! What a complicated-looking page (compared to what we've seen so far). The View system is very powerful, and so has many options. An exhaustive discussion of it is beyond the scope of this book. We'll only be using a few of the settings—which is much easier than it looks. While we are editing settings, the Live Preview area at the bottom of the page will be continuously updated to reflect our changes. It will show us what our View will look like, based on our current settings.

The Views page handles input from you differently to the pages that we've used so far. When you make a change to a field, and then save that change, AJAX (the technology, not the cleanser) is used to perform the update. This means that the change is recorded while you remain on the page, instead of the page reloading. The exception to this is the **Save** button at the bottom of the page, which indicates that you are saving the entire View, and not just a change in settings.

8. The first thing we'll address is a title for our view. This is the title that will be used when displaying the View to the site visitor. We'll click on the link that currently says **None** next to the heading **Title**.

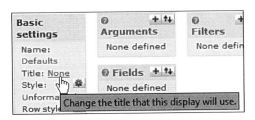

9. When we clicked on it, the little AJAX icon started spinning, and down between the View panel and the **Save** button, a dialog box opens. We'll enter our title into this, and then click on the **Update** button.

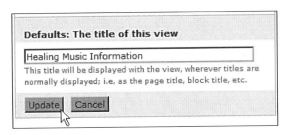

10. The next setting that we need to update is the **Row style**. Let's click on the plugin.

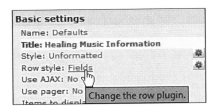

11. In the row dialog, we'll change the **Row style** from **Fields** to **Node**. This means that in each 'row' in our view there will be a piece of Node Content, and that the same engine that formats Node Content for a Story or Page display will be used to format each node in the View. Click on the **Update** button.

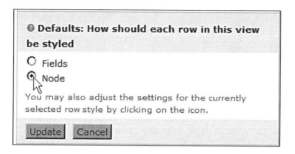

12. Because this is a new View, once we've updated the row style, we get a second dialog box (as seen the upcoming screenshot) in the same place on the screen. This one allows us to specify what we want to see for each node. By default, the teaser for the Node Content will be shown instead of the entire article. The links for entering a comment, and so on, will appear as well. We want only the teaser to show, so that we can fit several teasers on one page, and we also need the links, as the Read More link isn't visible otherwise. Click on the **Update** button.

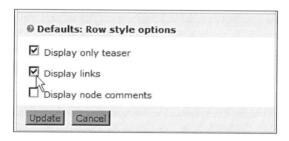

13. In the next dialog box we will select the **Distinct** checkbox. This setting prevents a node from being presented more than once. At the time of writing, this option does not always work. If your View is based on more than one criterion, and if more than one of the criteria apply to a piece of Node Content, then it could appear more than once. In our case, the View will be based on a single criterion, so we shouldn't have that problem. Click on the **Update** button.

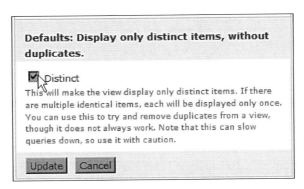

14. I'll now mention the next four settings. Although we're not going to use them, you might find them useful, depending on your requirements.

   ° **Access** — we're going to leave it set to the default setting (**Unrestricted**), but you can limit the access to the View so that, for example, only members can access it.

   ° **Header** and **Footer** — these settings allow you to create header text, which will be displayed above the rows of Node Content, and a footer, which be displayed below the rows. These are created in the same way as a Body, complete with a choice of Input format.

   ° **Empty text** — this setting allows you to define text to be shown in the event that there is no Node Content matching the View criteria.

   ° The next setting that we need to change is the **Sort criteria**. We need to click the plus sign, instead of the link.

15. Clicking the + button opens up a dialog box that lists all of the possible sort criteria. We can shorten the list, and by doing so make it easier to find the one that we want, by selecting **Node** from the **Groups** list box. We'll choose that because we will be sorting, based on how recently the Node Content was edited.

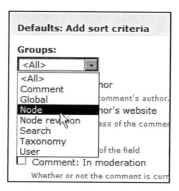

16. From the shortened list of sort criteria, we'll scroll down, and select the **Updated date** checkbox, and then click on the **Add** button.

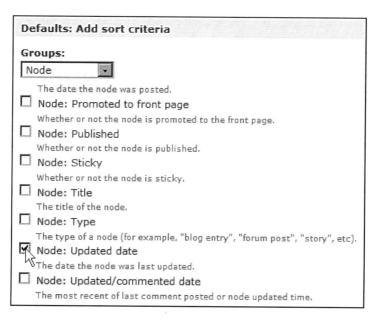

17. Once we've added the sort field, a new dialog box appears that allows us to refine the sort that we just chose. This dialog box is seen in the following screenshot. We want the most recent Node Content to appear first, so we will select **Descending** as the type of sort, and then click on the **Update** button.

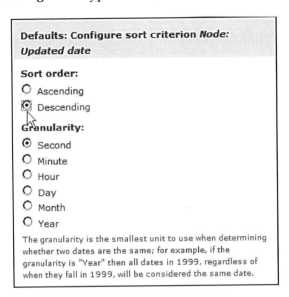

18. The final setting is really the meat of this particular View — the **Filters**. This setting is where we will define which Node Content to show. Filters can be thought of as selection criteria. For example, a filter that is commonly used is to ensure that the Node Content has been set to Published. We might also want to select only the Node Content published this year. Filters allow us to pare down our selection from 'all Node Content' to something more targeted. In our case, we're going to filter, based on the subject of our Node Content. Earlier we created a taxonomy vocabulary. We'll use the entries in it to determine which Node Content we want this View to show.

19. We'll begin by clicking on the + button, just as we did with Sort.

20. Here too, there is a **Groups** list box for our use. We'll select **Taxonomy** from it.

21. From the Taxonomy options, we'll select **Taxonomy: Term**, and then click on the **Add** button.

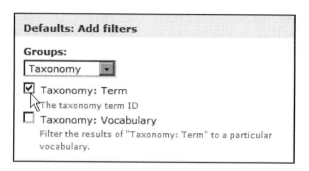

22. In the next dialog box, shown in the following screenshot, we will specify how we are going to use Taxonomy to filter our Node Content. We will select **Tags** as the **Vocabulary** (because we want to use a specific tag type), **Dropdown** as the **Selection type**, and then click on the **Update** button.

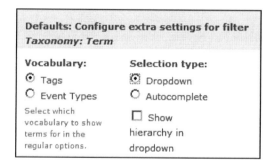

 There are a number of terms for the screen control that allows you to select from a list of choices that are stacked vertically in one control. The two most often used are 'dropdown' and 'pulldown', which are the types of list box that opens to show choices when the field is clicked on.

23. We now have a list box from which we can select terms (shown in the following screenshot). We could select multiple terms if we wanted to, but in this case, we're going to limit what Node Content we will be shown, by filtering on a specific term. We will retain the setting that our term **Is one of** the tags assigned to the Node Content in order to be chosen. We'll then select **healing music** from the list box, and then click on the **Update** button.

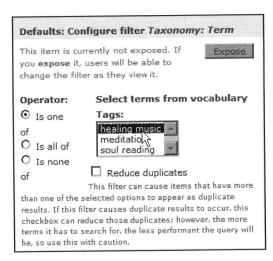

The three settings in the filter box can be confusing. This is their meaning:

- **Is one of** — is like searching with 'or' between terms when selecting more than one term. The Node Content will be selected as long as at least one of the terms assigned to it match what you select here.

- **Is all of** — is like searching with 'and' between the terms when selecting more than one term. Every term you select here must also be assigned to the Node Content for it to be selected. It doesn't matter if the Node Content has *more* terms than what you select here.

- **Is none of** — the term(s) that you select here must *not* be assigned to the Node Content in order for it to be selected.

24. At this point, it would appear that our View is complete. The following screenshot shows the settings as we have configured them to this point. We'll click on the **Save** button at this point, to protect our work.

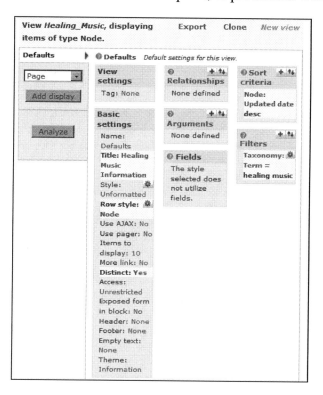

25. Saving the View leaves us on the same page, and we'll use this opportunity to make certain that we've done everything that we need to. The **Analyze** button, seen in the following screenshot, will check our settings, and let us know if something is amiss.

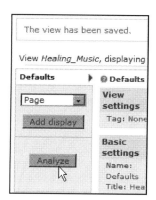

26. As it turns out, it's a good thing that we checked. Looking at the **View analysis** report that was generated when we clicked the **Analyze** button, there are two important actions that we neglected to take.

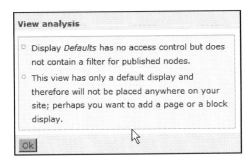

27. The first problem is that we neither specified neither an access control nor a filter for the **Published** nodes. This means that, for example, if we have Node Content that is not ready to be published, but meets the term criteria, the Node Content will be selected for this View, which could be very awkward. We can remedy this via access control, restricting access to this View based on permissions or user type. However, what we really want to do is make this View available to everyone, with the Node Content being only published content. Let's click on the + button next to the **Filters** field, and add a new filter.

28. From the **Groups** list, we'll select **Node**, this time. Then, we'll scroll down and select **Node: Published** from the list, and then click on the **Add** button.

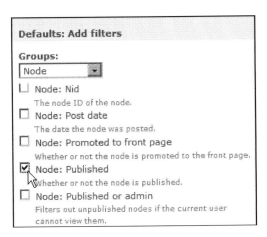

29. In the new dialog box that appears (shown in the following screenshot), we will specify that the node must be published in order to be selected, and then we click on the **Update** button.

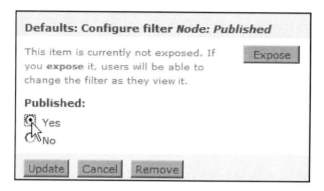

30. We can see in the screenshot below that our Filter settings have changed accordingly.

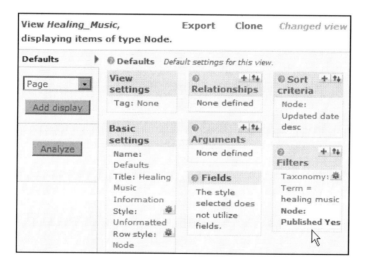

31. Let's turn our attention to the second item in the analysis report. You'll notice **Defaults** in the upper left of our View settings. With that being the only term showing, we've not actually committed this View to appear anywhere (such as in a Block or a Page). After all this work, we want the View to be seen! We want it to appear as a Page. Therefore, with the list box showing **Page**, we'll click on the **Add display** button.

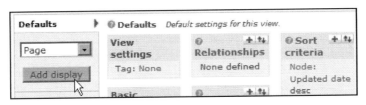

32. The upper-top left section of our page has now changed. In addition to **Defaults**, we see that **Page** is also listed. These are actually tabs. At the moment, the **Page** tab is selected, and we have an additional dialog box at the bottom of the page, as shown in the following screenshot. This points out to us that we have no **Path** assigned to this View yet. This is because the View is not based on a single piece of Node Content, so a **Path** must be assigned (although, between you and me, I don't know why the View title couldn't be used as a default). It also points out that there is no menu link that leads to this View, so a site visitor would have no way to access it. Let's address the former by clicking on **None**, which is a link.

33. In the dialog box that opens, we'll enter **healingmusic** as the path, and then click on the **Update** button. We can see the update recorded on the Page settings box, as shown in the screenshot below.

34. Next, we'll resolve the menu issue. In the same **Page settings** box, we'll click on the **No menu** option.

35. In the **Menu item entry** dialog box, we'll select **Normal menu entry** as the **Type**. The **Title**, which is what the menu link will show, is set to **Healing Music**. The **Description** is the tool tip text that will appear when the mouse is held over the link. Let's make this **Healing Music Information**. In the **Menu** list box, we'll select **Primary links**, which is our top menu. The **Weight**, which defines the relative placement of this link, will be set at **50**, in order to place this link after those that are already defined. Then, click on the **Update** button.

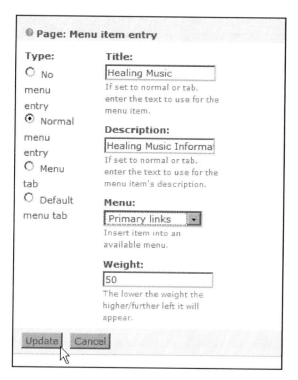

36. Having made these changes, let's run the analysis again. This time, the results are just what we want to see, as shown in following screenshot.

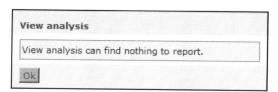

37. Finally, we can click on the **Save** button, and save our View. Let's go to the home page. Here we will see the new menu link. Hover your mouse over the link to read the description, and then click on it.

38. Here we are at our new View. As shown in upcoming screenshot, it contains two CD stories about **Healing Music**. As more Pages, Stories, Events and other types of Node Content are created that have the **Healing Music** tag, they will show up in this View.

So, why do we want a View? The short answer to this question is that without the View, we cannot have multiple Node Content items on a page or in a block where we can control the selection. In this example, we wanted a page that will allow us to present multiple pieces of Node Content of a subject matter of our choosing, and a View is the perfect choice for that. Behind the scenes, the creation of a View results in the generation of an SQL statement to draw the requested information from the database. In our case, this is Nodes that have a **Healing Music** tag. When we click on the menu link, the SQL statement is executed, and then each record, or Node, is sent to the same rendering engine that is used to display a Page or Story.

Another use for a View is to create a Block that contains changing but targeted information. For example, if we were to create a View for a block, and specify that it will contain a teaser for the most recent nodes, and limit it to showing only one node, then we have the makings of a 'Read the Latest advertisement' that will keep itself up-to-date automatically.

On Blogging

We've looked at Views, which gives us a means for displaying Node Content in a different way than Drupal normally gives us. Another example of presenting information to your visitors in a different way is a Blog. A blog is an online diary. Blogs can add richness and intimacy to a site by bringing the site visitors closer to the author. Blogs are meant to contain informal content, as opposed to the typical content found in a Story or a Page.

There are some administrative requirements in Drupal for establishing a blog or blogs. The specifics are beyond the scope of this book, but a summary is provided after the next activity. If you do not see **Blog entry** as a Node Content type in your admin menu, then it has not yet been enabled by the administrator, or your user role does not have the permissions to use it.

Activity 6.3: Creating a Blog entry

Let's now create a test Blog entry to explore the process of creating a blog.

1. From the admin menu, we'll select **Create content**, just as we did to create a Page and a Story.

2. On the **Create content** page shown in the following screenshot, we'll select the **Blog entry** option.

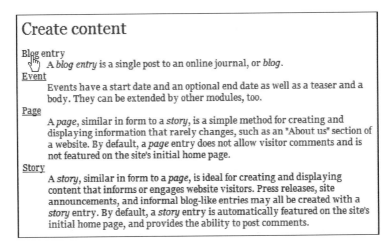

3. In the **Title** field, we'll simply enter **Test blog entry**.

4. In the **Tags** field, we'll type **he**, and Drupal will use AJAX to offer **healing music** as a suggestion, which we'll then select.

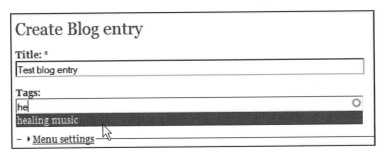

5. This is just an exercise to add an entry to an existing blog, and this blog entry will be deleted later. In the Body field, we'll just enter a sentence or two in order to have something to show.

6. Once we've entered the text, we'll click on the **Save** button.

7. Upon navigating to the front page, we can now see the new blog entry (shown in the upcoming screenshot). We have several options here. We can click on the title, which would take us to the full blog entry. However, in this case there is no more content to be seen. We can also click on the **taxonomy** link, which will take us to a page such as the View that we have created. There's also a link for the overall blog, which leads to a page of blog entries for this blog. Lastly, there should be a link to **Add new comment** (if not, then this capability has not been enabled). The ability to create comments is controlled in the permissions admin function. This ability can be turned on or off in general, and is controlled separately for each user role, or even for a specific piece of Node Content. We'll click on the **Add new comment** link.

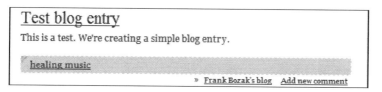

8. Clicking on the link has taken us to a page on which we can create a new comment. The name of the page is a bit misleading: **Reply to comment**. The comment we are replying to is actually the blog entry. The following screenshot shows the field entries that we make, before we click on the **Preview** button.

Reply to comment

> Test blog entry
>
> This is a test. We're creating a simple blog entry.
>
> healing music
>
> » Frank Bozak's blog   Add new comment

Reply

Your name: admin

Subject: Love this blog

Comment: *

Great blog entry!

Switch to plain text editor.
The ID for excluding or including this element is *blog@comment/reply*

9. The preview is then shown to us, and at this point we'll click on the **Save** button.

10. What you'll then see at the top of the screen depends on the permissions held by your current login. If you don't see the message shown in the upcoming screenshot, then it's because your user role has been given the permission to post comments without moderation, or because you are logged in as the site owner. Depending on the site settings, posted comments may appear immediately, or may be queued and awaiting approval from a user with the correct permissions.

> Your comment has been queued for moderation by site administrators and will be published after approval.

Let's take a look at how to approve a comment.

1. Go to the admin menu, and select the **Content management** option.

2. From the Content management page, we'll select the **Comments** option.

3. The initial screen displays the **Published comments**. We'll then click on the tab for the **Approval queue**.

4. The comment that we created (shown in the following screenshot) is here awaiting deletion, editing, or approval. We'll select the checkbox to its left, and as the choice in the list box is already set to **Publish the selected comments**, we'll simply click on the **Update** button.

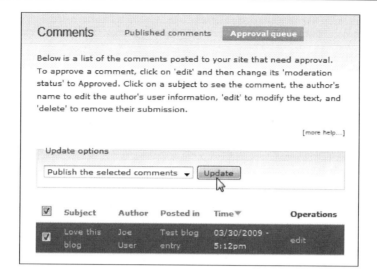

5. Now, upon returning to the front page, we'll see that the blog entry mentions a comment (pointed to by the mouse cursor in the following screenshot). The site visitor can click on the link to read it, or simply read the full blog entry that will be displayed along with the comments. You can also change the admin settings to show comments on the front page. However, we won't do that here, because they use up too much real estate, and are not essential to the site's purpose.

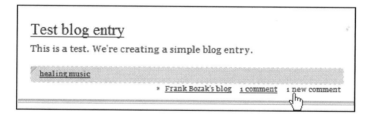

Setting up a Blog

Here is a brief summary of the admin steps that are necessary to enable blogs in Drupal 6.

1. On the Modules page, activate the **Blog** module.

2. [Optional] On the **User management** page, create a new user type, such as **Blogger**. You would need to do this if only a subset of registered (authenticated) users will be allowed to blog.

3. Also on the **User management** page, set the Blog permissions for each user type. These determine the type(s) of user that can create, edit, and delete blog entries.

4. Finally, again in user management permissions, set which type of user can post comments and which (if any) can do so without moderation.

Summary

In this chapter we have learned how to enliven our web sites with richer content. Along the way, we have learned about:

- **Blocks** — the tiny building blocks of a content-rich site
- **Views** — the grouping of Stories of similar content on a single page
- **Blogs** — a Web-based interactive diary

Through these activities we have learned how to:

- Create a Block as an advertisement to appear outside of the normal content area
- Create a View to display content for the selected taxonomy terms
- Create a blog entry, comment on it, and approve the comment

In Chapter 7, we will learn about managing a content site that involves a team with various responsibilities.

7
Supporting an Editorial Team

Up to this point, we've been working in an environment where a single person does the job of creating, editing, approving, and publishing. This works well with a small site and a low volume of content. However, where large sites and larger quantities of content prevail, there is often a team involved.

What you will learn

In this chapter, we will learn about some of the terminologies that Drupal provides for supporting team work, such as:

- **Roles** — defining types of users
- **Permissions** — defining capabilities for each role
- **Node Content types** — as they apply to Roles
- **Access Rules** — for those pesky misbehaving users

What you will do

In this chapter, you will:

- Create a team
- Add Roles to support the team
- Define new Node Content types
- Configure permissions to support the Roles
- Handle a former (and disgruntled) team member

The Creative team

Let's take a quick look at Drupal's jargon regarding teams.

- **Users** — the logins of the individuals that make up a team
- **Roles** — the different 'job descriptions' based on a person's responsibilities
- **Permissions** — the granting of authorization to perform a Drupal function

As the system administrator, you are authorized to perform any action within the Drupal environment, but you would not want every member of a team to have this absolute capability, or else you would soon have chaos.

Let's first create a team. Then, we will look at assimilating that team into the Drupal environment.

Our Creative team will be made up of individuals, each having one or more of the responsibilities mentioned below (Note: the titles are not Drupal terms):

- **Copy Writers** — are the writers of short articles
- **Feature Writers** — are the writers of long pieces, in which style matters as much as content
- **Ad Writers** — are the writers of internal and external advertising that will appear in blocks
- **Proofreaders** — are the reviewers who check pieces for spelling, grammar, and usage errors
- **Associate Editors** — are the reviewers that are concerned with style, readability, and continuity
- **Style Editors** — are responsible for the formatting of content
- **Graphic Artists** — are the creators of the illustrations and images that are used as copy
- **Senior Editor** — is responsible for the quality of all of the above
- **Moderator** — manages postings by site visitors, such as comments and blog posts
- **Blogger** — creates blog entries
- **Administrator** — addresses the aspects of the site unrelated to content

With our team assembled, let's move on to creating the roles in our site.

Roles

Drupal comes with three roles installed: **creator** (also known as userID1), **authenticated user** and **anonymous user**. Only the latter two are listed when assigning permissions, because the creator role can do everything, including things that you might not want the administrator to be able to do. It's best not to use the creator's login as the administrator login. A separate administrator role should be created and granted the appropriate permissions. So, looking at the list above, we will need to create roles for all of our team members. Creating roles in Drupal is a quick and easy process. Let's create them.

Activity 7.1: Creating Roles

The **Name** of the role is assigned as per the responsibilities of the team member.

1.   Login as the administrator.
2.   Select the **User management** option.
3.   Select the **Roles** option.
4.   Enter the name of the role in the text box, as shown in the following screenshot, and then click on the **Add role** button.

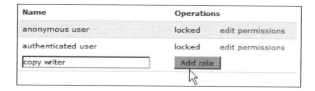

5.   We'll add the rest of the roles in the same way. After a couple of minutes, we have the entire team added, as seen in following screenshot.

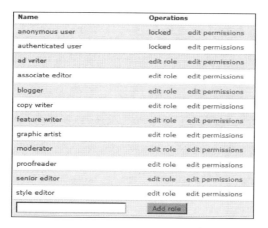

The edit role links are locked for **anonymous user** and **authenticated user**, because those roles should remain constant and never be edited or deleted.

Node Content types

The default installation of Drupal contains two Node Content types namely: Page and Story. Some modules, when activated, create additional Node Content types. One such example is the Blog entry, and another is an Event, which is used when using an event calendar.

 We're using the term Node Content to differentiate content nodes in Drupal, such as Pages and Stories, from other non-node types of content, such as Blocks, which is the generic term for anything on the page.

What is the purpose of having different Node Content types? If we want a feature writer to be able to create Features, then how do we accomplish that?

Currently, we have Stories and Pages as our Node Content types. So, if we give the Feature writer the ability to create a Page, then what differentiates that Page from any other Page on our site? If we consider a Page as a Feature, then anyone who can create a Page has created a Feature, but that's not right, because not every Page *is* a Feature.

Activity 7.2: Node Content for our Roles

Because we have role types that we want to limit to working with their respective Node Content types, we will need to create those Node Content types. We will assign a Node Content type of Feature for Feature Writers, Ads for Ad Writers, and so on. Let's create them.

1. From the admin menu, we'll select **Content management**.

2. On the **Content management** page, we'll choose **Content types.**

3. The Node Content types are listed, and from the top of the page we'll select **Add content type**.

4. We're going to start with the Feature writer, so in the **Name** field we'll enter **Feature**.

Name: *

Feature

The human-readable name of this content type. This text will be displayed as part of the list on the *create content* page. It is recommended that this name begin with a capital letter and contain only letters, numbers, and **spaces**. This name must be unique.

---

5. The next field, **Type**, determines the term that will be used to construct the default URL for this Node Content type. We'll enter **feature** as the text value for this field.

Type: *

feature

The machine-readable name of this content type. This text will be used for constructing the URL of the *create content* page for this content type. This name must contain only lowercase letters, numbers, and underscores. Underscores will be converted into hyphens when constructing the URL of the *create content* page. This name must be unique.

---

6. In the **Description** field, we'll enter a short description, which will appear next to the Node Content type's link on the admin page, as follows:

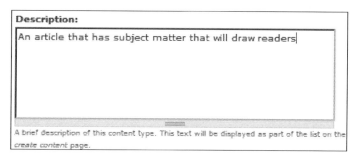

7. Next, we'll click on the **Workflow settings** link to display the additional workflow fields. When our Feature Writer completes a piece, it will not be published immediately. It will have to be proofread and undergo an editorial review. So, we'll deselect the **Published** and **Promote to front page** boxes.

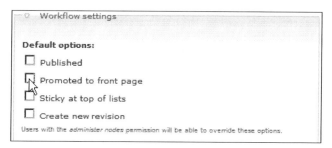

8. At this point we've configured the new Node Content type as per our needs, so we'll click on the **Save** button, and then we can see it listed, as shown in the screenshot below.

Feature	feature	An article that has subject matter that will draw readers		edit	delete

We already have a Node Content type of Blog entry, which was created by the Blog module. The only other Role that requires its own Node Content type is the Ad Writer. This is because the other Roles defined will only edit existing Node Content, as opposed to creating it. It is here that we run into trouble.

The pieces that are 'grabbed' by Drupal to appear (usually) at the center of the screen, which we have been referring to as Node Content, are nodes, whether a Page, a Story, or now a Feature. The small blocks that appear around the sides, or on top, or at the bottom, are Blocks. Because they are placed in those positions, and are not available for selection as Node Content, they are not nodes.

The Benefit of Blocks

When looking at a typical web page of a CMS site, you will see a main body area with Node Content, such as articles, and also small blocks of information elsewhere on the page, such as in the left and right margins, or along the top or bottom. The main content, nodes, are limited, as to where they appear. However, each of the blocks can be configured to appear on any or every page of the site. That is why ads are best created as blocks, so that they can be placed where they will be the most effective.

Nodes are created via the **Create content** function, and that function is available from the front page to anyone who is granted the permission. Using the admin menu is not necessary. On the other hand, blocks are created and edited from the **Block** page, which is an admin function.

Although we can grant that capability to a user without granting any other admin capabilities, it would be much better if we could have an Ad Writer create ads in the same way that they create other Node Content. The reason for this is that with nodes, separate permission can be given to create a node and to administer a node. With blocks, there is only one permission. You can create, edit, delete, and rearrange all of the blocks, or none. This opens the door to an accidental disaster. We don't want the Ad Writer doing anything but creating ad copy.

So, in order to address this concern, we've added a module to our site: **Node blocks**. This module allows us designate a Node Content type (other than Page and Story) to be used as a Block. With that in mind, let's create our final Node Content type.

Where can you find this module? This module, as well as other modules, can be found at `http://drupal.org/project/modules`. See *Appendix B* for a list of resources.

Activity 7.3—creating a Block Node Content type

We'll start by repeating Steps 1 to 3 from the previous activity.

1. In the **Title field**, we'll type in **Ad**.

2. In the **Type field**, we'll type in **ad**.

3. For the description, we'll enter **Advertisement copy that will be used as blocks**.

4. We'll click on **Workflow settings** and deselect **Published** and **Promoted to front page**, as we did with the Feature.

5. There is a new heading in this dialog, **Available as Block**, as seen in the following screenshot. This comes from the module that we've added. We'll select **Enabled**, which will make any piece created with this Node Content type available as a Block.

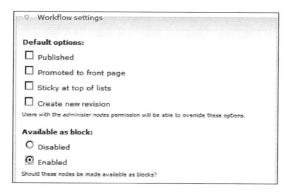

6. That's all we need to do, so now we'll save our new Node Content type.

Permissions

The way that we enable one user to do something that the other cannot is by creating different user types (which we have done), different Node Content types—where necessary—(which again has been done), and then assign permissions to the user types (which we'll do now).

The administrator will not be listed as a user type under Permissions, because if permissions were accidentally removed from the administrator, there might be no other user type that has the permissions to restore them.

Activity 7.4: Granting Permissions

Let's now assign to the members of the Creative team the Permissions that suit them best.

1. From the admin menu we'll select **User management**.

2. On the **User management** page we'll choose **Permissions**.

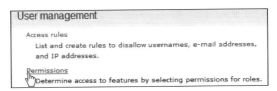

3. The screenshot below shows us the upper portion of the screen. There are numerous permissions, and we now have numerous User types, so the resulting grid is very large. Rather than step-by-step illustrations, I'll simply list each Role and the Permissions that should be enabled in the form of Heading → Permission.

- Ad Writer
    - ○ node module → access content
    - ○ node module → create ad content
    - ○ node module → delete any ad content
    - ○ node module → delete own ad content
    - ○ node module → edit any ad content
    - ○ node module → edit own ad content
    - ○ node module → view revisions
    - ○ fckeditor module → access fckeditor

Because of the number of Node Content types, each having several permissions as seen above, combined with the permissions being alphabetical by verb within the heading, instead of Content type, the necessary permissions are somewhat distant from each other and require scrolling to find them all.

- Feature Writer
    - ○ node module → access content
    - ○ node module → create feature content
    - ○ node module → delete any feature content
    - ○ node module → delete own feature content
    - ○ node module → edit any feature content
    - ○ node module → edit own feature content
    - ○ node module → view revisions
    - ○ fckeditor module → access fckeditor
- Blogger
    - ○ blog module → create blog entries
    - ○ blog module → delete own blog entries
    - ○ blog module → edit own blog entries
    - ○ node module → access content
    - ○ node module → view revisions
    - ○ fckeditor module → access fckeditor

- Associate Editor—The Associate Editor is concerned with content, which means editing it. The ability to create or delete content, to affect where the content appears, and so on, is not required for this Role.
  - ○ fckeditor module → access fckeditor
  - ○ node module → access content
  - ○ node module → edit any ad content
  - ○ node module → edit any feature content
  - ○ node module → edit any page content
  - ○ node module → edit any story content
  - ○ node module → revert revisions
  - ○ node module → view revisions
  - ○ path module → create URL aliases

- Copy Writer
  - ○ fckeditor module → access fckeditor
  - ○ node module → access content
  - ○ node module → create page content
  - ○ node module → create story content
  - ○ node module → delete own page content
  - ○ node module → delete own story content
  - ○ node module → edit own page content
  - ○ node module → edit own story content
  - ○ node module → view revisions

- Graphic Artist
  - ○ blog module → edit any blog entry
  - ○ fckeditor module → access fckeditor
  - ○ fckeditor module → allow fckeditor file uploads
  - ○ node module → access content
  - ○ node module → edit any ad content
  - ○ node module → edit any feature content
  - ○ node module → edit any page content
  - ○ node module → edit any story content

- Moderator
    - blog module → edit any blog entry
    - comment module → access comments
    - comment module → administer comments
    - fckeditor module → access fckeditor
    - node module → access content
    - node module → edit any ad content
    - node module → edit any feature content
    - node module → edit any page content
    - node module → edit any story content
- Proofreader
    - blog module → edit any blog entry
    - fckeditor module → access fckeditor
    - node module → access content
    - node module → edit any ad content
    - node module → edit any feature content
    - node module → edit any page content
    - node module → edit any story content
- Style Editor
    - block module → administer blocks
    - fckeditor module → access fckeditor
    - fckeditor module → allow fckeditor file uploads
    - node module → access content
    - node module → edit any ad content
    - node module → edit any feature content
    - node module → edit any page content
    - node module → edit any story content
- Senior Editor
    - block module → administer blocks
    - blog module → delete any blog entry
    - blog module → edit any blog entry
    - comment module → access comments

- ○ comment module → administer comments
- ○ fckeditor module → access fckeditor
- ○ fckeditor module → allow fckeditor file uploads
- ○ node module → access content
- ○ node module → delete any ad content
- ○ node module → delete any feature content
- ○ node module → delete any page content
- ○ node module → delete any story content
- ○ node module → delete revisions
- ○ node module → edit any ad content
- ○ node module → edit any feature content
- ○ node module → edit any page content
- ○ node module → edit any story content
- ○ node module → revert revisions
- ○ node module → view revisions
- ○ path module → create URL aliases
- ○ view module → access all views
- ○ view module → administer views

With that, we have assigned the required permissions to all of our team members, which will allow them to do their jobs, but keep them out of trouble! However, what do you do when someone intentionally gets into trouble?

The disgruntled team member

So, we've been marching along as one big happy team, and then it happens. Someone gets let go, and that someone isn't happy about it, to say the least.

Of course, we'll remove that person's login, but there is public access to our site as well, in the form of comments. Is there a way for us to stop this person from looking for ways to annoy us, or worse? Yes!

Activity 7.5: Blocking

Let's now perform the tasks necessary to keep disgruntled employees (and trouble-makers) at bay.

1. From the admin menu, select **User management**.
2. On the User management page, we'll select the **Access rules** option.
3. We'll choose the **Add rule** option on the **Access rules** page.

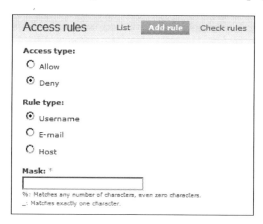

4. On the **Add rule** page, we have the option to deny access to a user, email address, or host.

    ○ The username and email address options will block someone from registering, but will not affect someone already registered.

    ○ The host name will stop anyone with that host name from accessing the system at all.

    ○ Wild cards can be used: % will match any number of characters, and _ will match one character.

    ○ **Allow** rules can be used to give access to someone who would otherwise be blocked by a host or wild card rule.

5. In our case, let's say that the disgruntled former team member is spamming our comments from a host called `spamalot.com`, and is doing it from many emails. The first thing we want to do is create a 'Deny' rule that will deny access to anyone from that host, as shown in the following figure, and then click on the **Add rule** button.

6. We're also going to create an email deny rule for %**@spamalot.com**. We shouldn't have to (as we've already denied the host, which in turn would include all of the emails from that host), but we need to, because the rules testing logic ignores that hierarchy at this time.

7. Let's also say that we've received an email from someone whose email address is **its_not_me@spamalot.com**, who would like to be a member of our site, and we verify that this person is not our former team member. In such a scenario, we will need to create an **Allow** rule, as shown in the following screenshot, so that this person can get past our previous **Deny** rule.

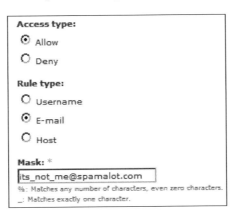

8. Our rules now appear, as shown below, when we click on the **List** button, which is at the top of the page.

Access type ▲	Rule type	Mask	Operations
deny	host	%spamalot%	edit delete
deny	e-mail	%@spamalot.com	edit delete
allow	e-mail	its_not_me@spamalot.com	edit delete

9. It's always good to check and make certain that we've created the rule(s) correctly. If we don't do this, then we might inadvertently block the wrong users. Let's click on the **Check rules** tab at the top of the **Access rules** page.

10. In the email box, we'll first try **disgruntled@spamalot.com**.

> The e-mail address *disgruntled@spamalot.com* is not allowed.

11. Next, we'll try **its_not_me@spamalot.com**.

> The e-mail address *its_not_me@spamalot.com* is allowed.

In this last activity we have created some access rules. Drupal uses these access rules to determine who can and cannot access the site. In some cases, you may be having difficulty with a particular user adding comments to your site. Of course, if you set comments to require moderation, then the questionable ones won't appear, but it can still be a pain having to review a steady stream of them. In that case, you can block a specific user. You might be having difficulty with comments from more than one user at a given email domain. You can, if you like, block everyone from that location. On the other hand, your site might be meant for users of a particular domain, perhaps a university. In that case, you can allow users from that domain and only them.

Summary

In this chapter we learned about:

- Roles—defining types of users
- Permissions—defining capabilities for each role
- Node Content types—as they apply to Roles
- Access Rules—for those pesky, misbehaving users

These features have been explained and learned with the help of activities where we have:

- Created a team
- Added Roles to enable the team
- Defined new Node Content types to suit the requirements of some team members
- Configured permissions to support the Roles and Node Content types
- Handled a former (and disgruntled) team member

In Chapter 8, we will learn about submitting content from outside the web site.

8
Offline Content Creation

For most of the content that we've been creating in our activities, we've been typing directly into the Body text box on the Drupal site. It's certainly an easy way to create content, but is not always practical. Let's take a look at some solutions. Drupal has an ever-expanding wealth of add-on modules that are available for extended and/or enhanced functionality, and we'll make use of some of them.

What you will learn
In this chapter, you will learn how to:

- Use text content created outside of Drupal
- Blog using third-party blogging tools
- Create and edit Node Content via email

What you will do
In this chapter, you will:

- Create formatted content in a text editor and create Node Content from this
- Create a blog entry using the Blog API with Windows Live Writer
- Create and edit content via email, using the Mailhandler module

Creating content offline
Sometimes, we'd like to use the grammatical and formatting tools available in an application such as **MS Word** or **OpenOffice** to create content, instead of typing directly into Drupal (the reason being that an Internet connection may not always be available).

Activity 8.1: Pasting lightly-formatted text

Cutting and pasting is an activity that most computer users are familiar with. Even so, there are a couple of considerations when doing it into Drupal, and using rich text. Let's give it a try!

1. Let's create some formatted text. Pretty much any text editor will do. We'll be using OpenOffice here, since that's what I'm using right now. We'll just create two paragraphs of lightly-formatted text (indentation, bullets, italics, and so on), as shown below.

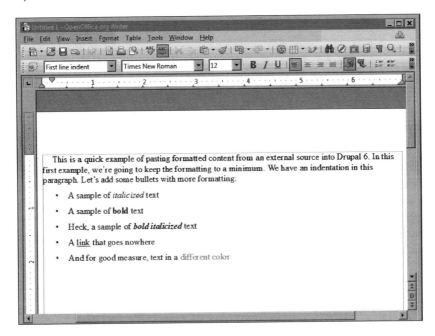

2. Next, we'll select the Create content option from the Admin menu, and create a new Story.

At some point you'll want to start remembering the URLs for common Drupal activities. To create Node Content, simply append `/node/add` to your domain name.

3. We'll simply enter **Activity 8.1** in the Title field.

4. Let's turn off the Rich Text Editor in the Body text box (if it's active). Then we'll copy the original text, and paste it into the text box. The following screenshot shows the result—our text with absolutely no formatting at all!

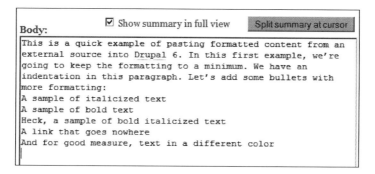

5. So, that was what we didn't want to happen. I showed it to you so that you would know that, but also because sometimes you do want to strip the formatting, and that is how to do it. Let's reactivate the FCKeditor (the Rich Text Editor).

Pasting from Word

Depending on which version of MS Word you are using, the Rich Text Editor that you are using, and how your text has been formatted, pasting it into the body box can result in squeaky-clean HTML, or a mess, even though both will look the same. If you look at the text using the editor's **Source** button, or by turning off the editor, then you might be surprised to see seemingly endless additional HTML tags.

6. The text is still on our clipboard, so we don't need to recopy it. We're going to click on the icon for pasting from Word, as shown in the following screenshot:

Although the icon refers to MS Word, it can be used with other text editors as well.

7. We receive a pop-up window into which we will paste the copy. When we paste it, we see that the formatting is correct in the window.

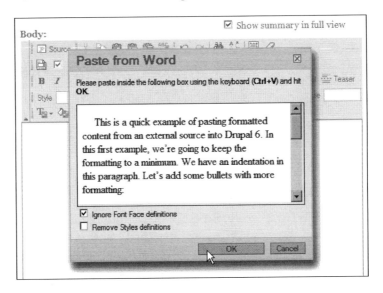

8. We'll click on the **OK** button, which will insert the copy into the body text box. We then see something interesting — the indentation disappears. We'll need to add it back manually. Aside from that, when we **Preview** the Story, we see, as shown in the following screenshot, that the formatting is intact.

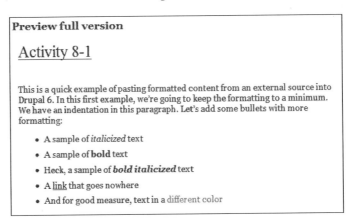

 There are so many different combinations of text editors and browsers that quirks are bound to happen when switching between them. Never assume that a task of pasting formatted text will be flawless.

Blogging

Blogging is meant to be a process where a blogger easily creates postings for the blog. Having to go into Drupal to create the entries isn't a particularly smooth process. There are easier ways to blog.

We're going to make use of the **Blog API** module, which has been enabled and configured by our administrator. This module allows a blogger to create a blog posting on a laptop, desktop, or smart phone, and post it directly to the blog. The permissions have been set in Drupal to allow my user ID this access, and to be able to create the Node Content type of Blog via the module. Our administrator has downloaded **Windows Live Writer**, and configured it to connect to the site. This application will allow us to create blog posts directly from our desktop, and post them on the web site. We're ready to go.

Activity 8.2: Creating a Blog entry remotely

Let's now perform the task of adding a blog entry to our Drupal web site from a remote location.

1. We'll run Windows Live Writer. As you can see in the following screenshot, the site name appears in the upper-right corner, showing us that we're configured and ready to go.

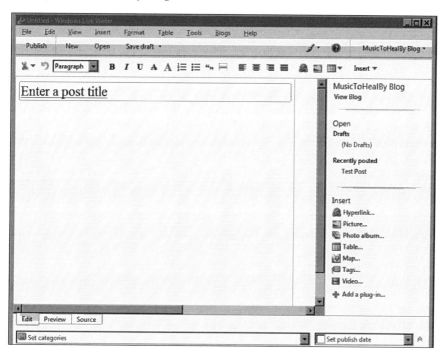

2. We'll enter a title, as shown in the following screenshot:

A Doggy Moment

3. Then we'll create the blog entry—anything will do. An example is shown in the following screenshot.

A Doggy Moment

I had a great day today...chased a *rabbit*, got some *table food*, had a couple *naps*, went for a *walk*. Just one of those days when everything seems to go right! I think I'll go do some meditation now.

4. At the bottom of the screen is a **Preview** tab, which allows us to preview the post as it will look in the Drupal theme, as shown in the following screenshot.

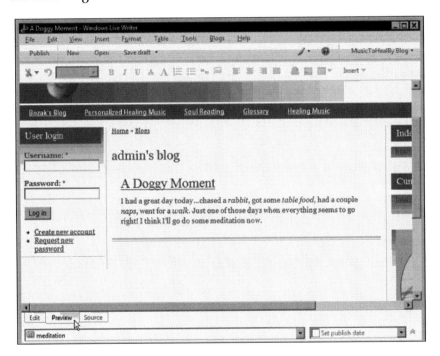

5. Going back to the **Edit** tab, we'll click on the **Categories** option at the bottom and add a category. The categories were downloaded by the software from the Tag list that we created way back in Chapter 5. As the blog entry refers to meditation, we'll select the **meditation** category.

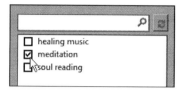

6. With everything ready, we'll click on the **Publish** button.

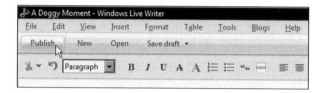

7. Our blog entry is posted, and we're automatically taken to the web site to view the new blog posting, as seen in the following screenshot.

There are various tools available for the PC and Mac for blogging. Any tool that offers Movable Type API, MetaWeblog API, or Blogger Data API, for example, can communicate with the Drupal's **Blog API** module. The important thing to remember when configuring the tool on your computer or phone is that the address to give it for the blog will be the domain URL plus /xmlrpc.php. So, for example, for our **Music To Heal By** site, the address will be http://musictohealby.com/xmlrpc.php.

Node Content via email

Creating the Blog entry in the previous example was fairly simple, but it still required that the blogger has a computer or smart-phone available, with some blogging software installed. However, there is a method that demands less from the blogger. These days, people have easy access to email, and we're going to use email, and nothing else, to create Node Content on our site.

Another useful add-on module for Drupal is Mailhandler. Our admin installed and configured it, and then created an email address to which any email sent will be considered as new Node Content. With that done, let's create a new Story.

Activity 8.3: Using email to create a Story

In this activity, we shall create a Story on our Drupal web site via email.

1. We'll use our email client to send an email to the mail address that our admin has created for us.

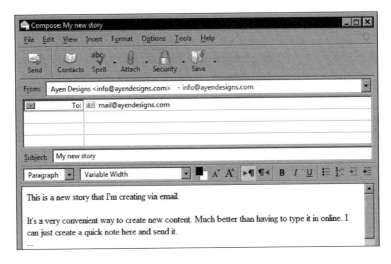

2. We then go to our admin menu and select **Mailhandler** from the **Content management** menu (shown in the following screenshot). Remember, Mailhandler is an add-on module. If it has not been installed and enabled on your site, then you will not see it in the admin menu.

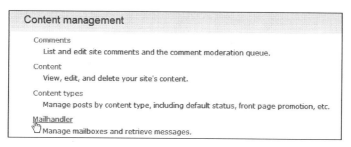

3. On the **Mailhandler** page, we see the mailbox entry that the administrator has created for us. The mailbox exists where all of the other emails for this domain are. It's not in any way a special mail address. It's just that we will have Drupal retrieve the messages from it. No mail messages from this mailbox have been retrieved as yet, so we'll click on the **Retrieve** operation.

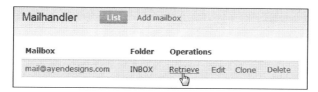

4. The Mailhandler retrieves whatever messages are waiting (as seen in the following screenshot), whenever it is instructed to. It can be instructed to do so manually, as we just did, or automatically, as a cron job.

cron

Many functions in Drupal depend on repeated execution for their success. This includes indexing the terms in the content for use in the **Search** function and in generating tags, retrieving new News Feeds (if they're being used for content), checking whether newer versions of Drupal and modules are available, and retrieving email as we just did above. The Linux utility, cron, is used to schedule the automated execution of an application or Web page. With Drupal, the admin would schedule cron to run `cron.php` as often as needed.

5. The result of the retrieval is given in a status message, as shown in the following screenshot.

6. When we browse to the **Content management | Content** page, we see the new Story listed with the title that we have given it.

7. Finally, let's click on the article's name, and see the final result.

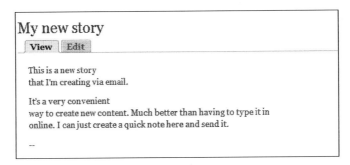

Even though we have created a Story in this example, the Mailhandler can be used to create any Node Content type that it has been enabled for. Simply putting **type: blog** in the message will create a blog entry, comment, or a forum post on the web page. Creation is not the only thing that we can do. We can also update Node Content too. Let's give it a try.

Activity 8.4: Using email to edit Node Content

Let's now use an email to edit a Node Content on the Drupal web site.

1. The steps in this activity will be the same as those in the previous activity, but our content will be slightly different, as will be the results. We'll begin by creating a new email message. This time we're going to use an email client that supports Rich Text. Here we'll use Yahoo Mail, as shown in the following screenshot.

Editing content via email requires that the email address configured in Drupal is associated with someone who has the permissions necessary to edit that node.

Mailhandler message format

In the message above, there are a few things to note:

- The subject will be used to replace the current title.
- Prior to the actual content, there are Mailhandler commands. The format is **command: value**, one per line, and you need to make sure that there is a space present between the command and the value.
- The **nid** command provides the node ID of the Node Content to be edited. This is the **nid** that appears in the URL, when editing online, or when hovering one's mouse over the `edit` link for that node in the list of Node Content, or when looking at the line below the Body box on the edit screen, which identifies the include link. In this case it is **30**.
- The **type** command identifies the Node Content type. In this case it is a Story.
- The **promote** command tells Mailhandler to promote this Node Content to be usable on the front (home) page.
- Also note that we have selected a phrase, underlined it, and made it bold.

2. After mailing our message, we'll repeat Steps 8 to 12 from the previous activity.

3. This time, when we view our Node Content list, we'll see our Story listed with the new title, as shown in the screenshot below.

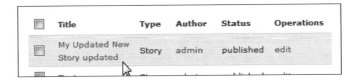

4. We can click on the **edit** operation to view the updated text, but instead, as we've promoted it, let's just look at the front page to see it, as shown in the following screenshot.

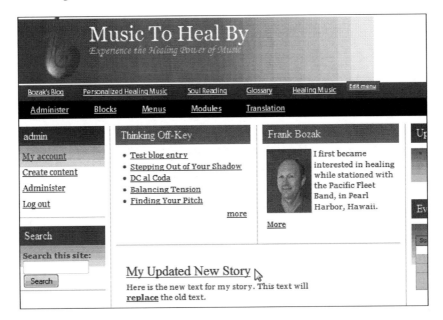

5. As you may have noticed, something odd has happened to the formatting. The title changed, the body changed, but instead of the words 'will replace' being formatted, only the word **replace** has been. This is a glitch at the time of writing, and may be fixed by the time that you try it. If not, then note that there may be some final polishing required online, if you're going to format the text.

Summary

In this chapter, we have learned about:

- Using text content created outside of Drupal
- Blogging using third-party blogging tools
- Creating and editing Node Content via email

These topics have been learned with the help of activities where we have:

- Created formatted content in a text editor, and created Drupal content from this
- Created a Blog entry using the Blog API with Windows Live Writer
- Created and edited a Story via email, using the Mailhandler module

A
Installing Drupal

In this book, the examples are based on a web site running on Drupal version 6. This Appendix shows the steps involved in setting up a new Drupal site.

Each web server is different in terms of the tools used for account and database manipulation, and so on. Therefore, it is likely that some of the steps that follow will differ in your case, but the essentials will remain the same.

The installation is divided among the following sections:

1. Determining if the hosting account meets spec
2. Downloading Drupal 6.x
3. Creating the database
4. Installing Drupal

Determining if the hosting account meets spec

Drupal has certain environmental requirements that need to be met in order to operate properly. Before going through the time and effort to install it, check with the server administrator to ensure that the following points are all true:

- Web server—Apache 1.3 or 2.x (it is possible to run Drupal on Microsoft IIS, but there are so many caveats that it isn't worth the effort)
- PHP 5.2 or higher
- mysql, mysqli or pgsql enabled in PHP

- PHP settings
  - `memory_limit: 64M` (some hosting accounts do not allow the memory to be overridden from the default 16M, so be careful)
  - `register globals: Off`
  - `session.save_handler: user`
  - `error_reporting: E_ALL`
  - `safe_mode: Off`
  - `session.auto_start: 0`
  - `.htaccess AllowOverride enabled`
- MySQL 4.1 or higher *or* PostgreSQL 7.4 or higher

Downloading Drupal 6.x

Once the environmental settings have been verified, we can proceed to the task of downloading the Drupal installation files.

1. Navigate to the `drupal.org/project/drupal` page. This page will look similar to the screenshot below.

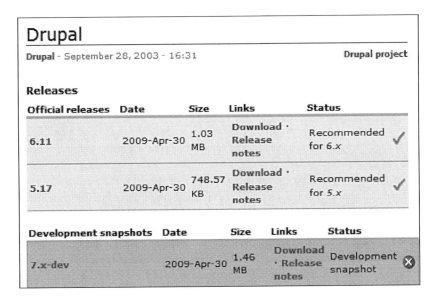

2. Download whichever version 6.x is shown in green (at the time of writing it was 6.11), and save the file (`drupal-6.11.tar.gz`) on your computer, but don't forget to make a note of where you put it.

3. What you do next will depend on whether you have **shell** access to your hosting account, or just FTP. If shell access is available, then skip to Step 7.

   The problem with uploading the file via FTP is that once you have done that, you will have no way to 'unzip' it. It will be easier to do that on your local computer, and then upload the resulting files via FTP.

4. Do a Web search for 'free gzip tar utility'. A good one is **7-zip**. You will first want to extract from the `.gz` file that you have downloaded, such as `drupal-6.11.tar.gz`. This will leave you with a single, new file, named `drupal-6.11.tar` (without the `.gz`).

5. Use your utility to unarchive the `.tar` file (known as a 'tar-ball'). This will leave you with a directory called `drupal-6.11`, in which the Drupal file system can be found.

6. Connect via FTP to the location where you want the files to be uploaded. Make sure that you are in the actual directory where you want to them to be placed (usually a directory named `public_html` or `www` inside the domain directory). Here, you want to upload all of the files within the Drupal directory, but not the directory itself. If you are running a FTP utility like **FileZilla**, then you can double-click on the Drupal directory to open it. Then select everything inside it and drag it all at once, and drop them onto the directory into which they should be placed (such as `public_html` or `www`). Skip to step 13.

7. (From step 3) Upload the `tar.gz` file to the directory in which your Drupal installation will reside in your domain, such as `public_html` or `www`.

8. Navigate in your shell to the directory where you put the file.

9. Enter the shell command `tar zxvf drupal-6.11.tar.gz` (or whatever your filename is).

10. You will now have all of the files unpacked, but they are not quite in the right place. They have been put in a directory with the same name as the file, but you don't want that directory between the domain root and all of the files. The files need to be moved 'up' one level (out of the directory in which they are now).

11. Enter the shell command `mv * ../` to move the files.

12. Drupal provides a default configuration file. We need to make a copy of it, which will then be used for our installation. In your FTP tool or your shell, navigate to the folder `sites/default/` and make a copy of the file `default.settings.php`. You should then rename it to `settings.php`.

13. The final directory structure can be seen in the following screenshot.

[This structure reflects version 6.11; other versions may vary.]

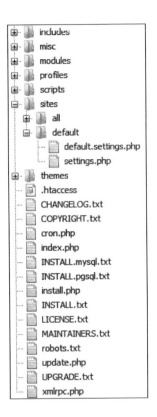

Creating the database

When running the Drupal installation, it expects a database to already exist, so we'll create one.

There's little to creating a database other than running the appropriate tool, such as MySQL, and giving the database a name and a password. Make a note of these, because you'll need this information in the next step. You'll also need to know the name of the database user, which on many systems is the same as the database. If you're using something like WAMP on a PC, then the database user might simply be root.

The final piece of information needed will be the database server. Again, if you're running the server on your workstation, or a dedicated server, the database server might just be localhost. If you're on a shared hosting account, then you'll need to click on the icon near the database name to get information, and make a note of the database server address, which will look like a long domain name. We're going to name our database drupal_6_11. You should have a list ready to use during the installation that looks something like this:

- User name: root   (don't use this on a real system)
- Password: MyDbPass123$ (don't make it easy)
- DB Name: drupal_6_11
- DB Server: mydbserver001.myserverdomain.net

Installing Drupal

Once the installation files have been uploaded to the root directory, and the database has been created, it's time for the Drupal installation to begin.

1.   We begin the installation of Drupal by navigating in our browser to the same directory into which we put it, such as http://mydomain.com or http://localhost. The first screen will look like the screenshot shown below. On the left-hand side you should see a progress list. Here, you can choose to install Drupal in a language other than the default option of English, but we'll click on the **Install Drupal in English** option.

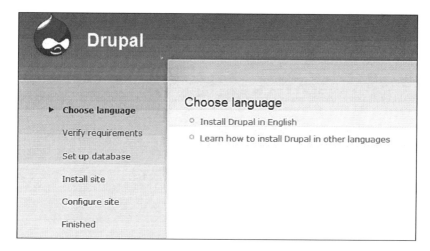

2. The next step is to provide the database information. As mentioned earlier, Drupal expects the database to exist. We'll fill in the information (as seen in the screenshot below), and then click on the **Save and continue** button.

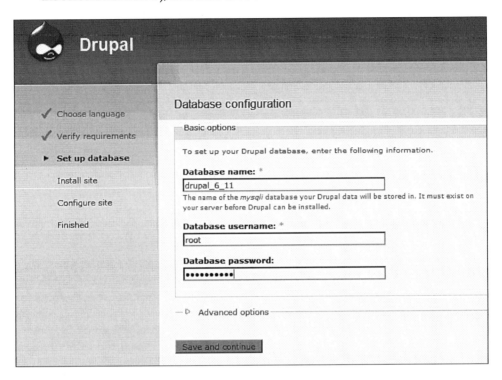

3. And away we go! As shown in upcoming screenshot, Drupal will now begin installing itself. It creates the tables and initial records in the database.

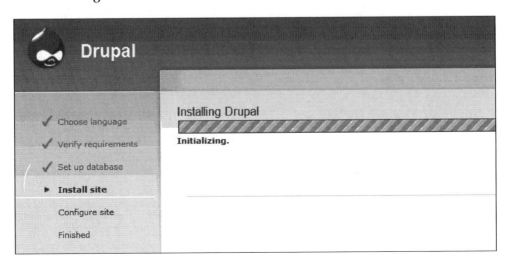

4. During the installation, you might see progress information, as shown next, but the installation is so quick that the numbers will flash by in a moment.

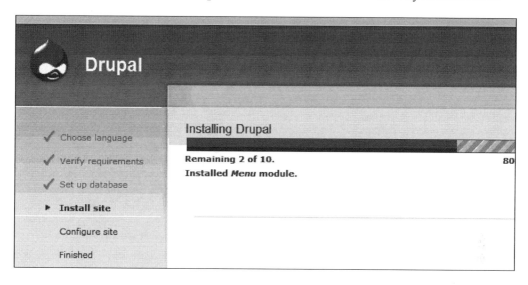

5. Once the file installation has completed, Drupal will prompt you for the configuration information in order to update the skeleton configuration file that you copied earlier. Let's take a look at the entries on this screen:

- ○ The **Site name** will default to the name of your web server. Change it to the name that you want to give the site.

- ○ The **Site email address** will be the address that the site will send emails from to new users, such as info@mydomain.com or webmaster@mydomain.com.

- ○ The **Username** is the name that will be used for the super-administrator (the one who can do anything to the site).

- ○ The **E-mail address** here is the one belonging to the user that we have just named.

- ○ **Password** is the password for this user. Drupal will tell you how secure it feels the password is: **Low**, **Medium** or **High**. Using a mix of upper and lowercase characters, numbers, and/or a symbol like '$' will make the password more secure.

- Next, we will identify the **Timezone** in which the server is located. The time zone is based on Greenwich Mean Time (GMT) being 0. Therefore, for example, New York, which is five hours behind Greenwich, England, would be in the -0500 time zone, while Paris, which is an hour past Greenwich, would be in +0100.

- I would recommend always using **Clean URLs**. Normally, the URL for a piece of content on Drupal might be something like `mydomain.com/index.php?q=42`, where `42` is the ID number of that piece of content. This kind of URL is confusing for site visitors, and isn't great for search engines either. Turning on **Clean URLs** would make the URL suffix `/node/42`, which is a little better. If you also enable the **Path** module, then you can then assign whatever URL suffix you'd like, such as `/about-our-company`.

- The final question on this page is whether Drupal should automatically check for updates, and see if there are any available for it and/or the modules that you install. I normally recommend enabling this, since often there are security updates released. That said, when updates are available, Drupal will throw up a pink warning box in the back end, indicating that there are updates available, and that the world might end if you don't use them. If you would like to schedule your updates without having nervous people suggesting it to you, then don't have updates done automatically.

The completed configuration page will look similar to the following screenshot. We can now click on the **Save and continue** option.

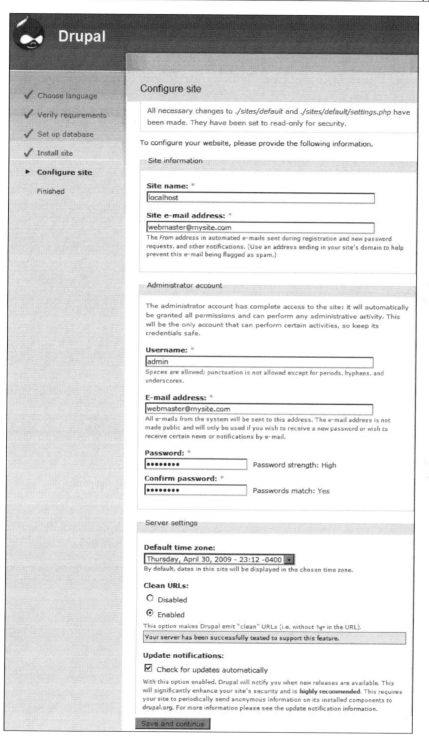

6. At this point, the installation is complete, as indicated by the page shown in the screenshot.

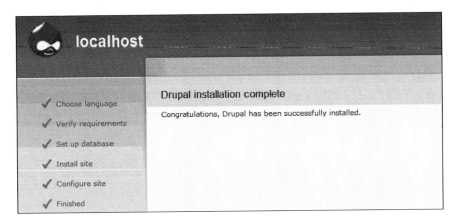

7. The only thing left that we need to do is to see our new front (home) page. By going to the original address again, instead of receiving the installation screen, we receive a page as follows:

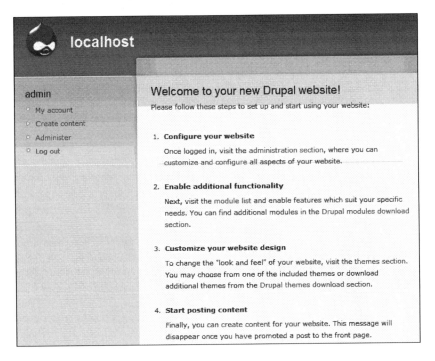

8. Now it would be a good idea to delete the install.php file, and the installation directory from our site's root directory.

B
Where to Find...

Drupal is a bit like the Constitution. It has a strong foundation that is holding up a framework, which is constantly growing. It is unlikely that you will create a site with Drupal and never add functionality to it, or need help, or require updates, and so on, as long as the site is in use.

The following is a list of resources aimed at making the continued use of your site easier.

Where to find help

There are a few different levels of help available. Keep in mind that Drupal is a free product, and as such no one owes you any help. With that said, the Drupal community is large and friendly, and help can easily be found.

Low-priority help

If you have a question that doesn't require an immediate response, then you can start by Googling your question (include 'Drupal' in the keywords), or by performing a search at the Drupal web site: `drupal.org`.

If you cannot find an answer there, or just hate reading 50 articles in the hope that one will be even slightly related to your question, then you can try searching the Drupal forum. If your question hasn't been asked and answered already, then you can post it. The Drupal forum is located at `drupal.org/forum`.

Medium-priority help

If you would prefer a more timely response, or think that your question would better be served by a dialog, rather than emails, then you can try the Drupal chat channels. If you have not used **IRC (Internet Relay Chat)** before, then it might take a little getting used to, but for the most part, it's like being in any chat room, except that everything said is related to the channel name.

You should start by downloading a chat client, such as **Chatzilla**, which is a free IRC client that ties into Firefox.

The main things to remember when in a technical chat channel:

Don't say 'hi' and wait for a response. Add your question on the same line.

Don't ask if you can ask a question—just ask!

Make your question concise. You can add the details afterwards. You're apt to get more attention if your question is one or two short sentences rather than a long screed.

Don't copy and paste a bunch of code or error messages, etc. If you need to provide that kind of information, then navigate your browser to `pastebin.com` (for text) or `imagebin.com` (for images) and paste it there. Then copy the link you're given and paste the link in the chat.

Be polite! These people don't 'work for' Drupal. You're asking for 'customer service' from someone who is a knowledgeable product user, not an employee of a company from which you purchased something.

High-priority help

High-priority help comes in the form of paid assistance. There is a plethora of knowledgeable Drupal developers out there, but please, please, please don't let someone you don't know touch your site. Use a consulting company with a good reputation, such as `AyenDesigns.com`. Get references and check them, or use a moderated job site, such as `Elance.com` or `Rentacoder.com`, to obtain assistance. If you use your cousin's friend who's good with computers, then you're asking for what you get.

ALWAYS make a complete backup of your web site and the database before letting someone touch it. Don't rely on the web hoster's backup. If your site gets trashed because you let your cousin's friend 'fix' it, then the web hoster will probably charge you a hefty fee to restore it from their backup.

Finding documentation

Unfortunately, documentation is the thing that everyone hates to do, especially if they're not being paid to do it. The documentation for Drupal is fairly extensive, but there are some holes. However, when you do find a hole, it's usually easily filled by other sources, such as the many blogs that you can find via your favorite search engine. The Drupal documentation can be found at `drupal.org/handbooks`.

Finding modules

Modules are one of the main building blocks of Drupal. Whereas Views are considered the building blocks of content, modules are the building blocks of feature richness. Modules are found at `drupal.org/project/modules`. When browsing through the modules, take note of the correct version. For example, if you are running a version of Drupal 6, which means you are running a 6.x version, then be sure that the module that you are considering is offered for Drupal 6, and that version is coded with a green background, meaning that it is a release which is ready for production use. The following is a list of the add-on modules that were used in this book. Each can be found at `drupal.org/project/modulename`, where `modulename` is replaced by one of the modules given below:

- Cumulus
- Event
- FCKEditor
- IMCE
- Mailhandler
- Nodeblock
- SWFTools
- Tagadelic
- Views

Finding themes

Themes are what will make your Drupal site look different from everyone else's Drupal site. Themes can be free or commercial. The best place to start your search for a theme is on the Drupal web site, at `drupal.org/project/Themes`. You can also use your favorite search engine to find many themes. If you cannot find something that's quite what you're looking for, then you can pay a web designer to have a theme custom-developed for you. Make certain that the designer has specifically done Drupal work before. Being able to design a slick home page isn't good enough, because, as you have seen, Drupal has functional areas on the page, and you cannot simply take just any web page design and superimpose it on Drupal.

Finding Packt guides

A few Packt guides that will help you enhance your Drupal web site are as follows:

Flash with Drupal

`http://www.packtpub.com/build-flash-applications-with-drupal-6/book`

Drupal Multimedia

`http://www.packtpub.com/create-multimedia-website-with-drupal/book`

Drupal 6 Themes

`http://www.packtpub.com/drupal-6-themes/book`

Building Powerful and Robust Websites with Drupal 6

`http://www.packtpub.com/drupal-6-create-powerful-websites/book`

Index

user management area, users 14
user management area, user settings 14
Drupal front end
about 10
content area 11
header area 11
left navigation area 11
top navigation area 11
Drupal web site
blogging 151
content, creating offline 147-150
Node content editing, email used 156-158
story creating, email used 154-156

E

email
using, to create Node Content 156-158
using, to create story 154-156

F

FCKeditor 52

G

graphic artists, creative team 132

H

help, levels
high-priority help 172
low-priority help 171
medium-priority help 172
hosting account spec, determining 161, 162
href 45
HTML
about 49
used, for enhancing layouts 64, 65
hyperlink reference. *See* **href**
Hyper Text Markup Language. *See* **HTML**

I

image
in content, working with 45
inserting 49, 50
link, creating 50-52

uploading 46-49
using, in content 45
include file
creating 67-69
input format, content form fields
about 27
filtered HTML (default) 27
full HTML 27
PHP code 27
installing
Drupal 165-170
Internet Relay Chat. *See* **IRC**
IRC 172

L

layouts
enhancing, CSS used 65
enhancing, HTML used 64, 65
link
anatomy 44
creating, within Node Content 41

M

Mailhandler module 154
menu settings, content form fields
menu link title 28
parent item 28
weight 28
modules
finding 173

N

Node Content
about 19
audio, embedding 52-54
audio content, adding 52
Block Node Content type, creating 137
editing, email used 156-158
flash movie, embedding 60, 62
for roles 134-136
story creating, email used 154-156
taxonomy, assigning 84-89
types 19, 134
video, embedding 60

Packt Open Source Project Royalties

When we sell a book written on an Open Source project, we pay a royalty directly to that project. Therefore by purchasing Drupal 6 Content Administration, Packt will have given some of the money received to the Drupal project.

In the long term, we see ourselves and you—customers and readers of our books—as part of the Open Source ecosystem, providing sustainable revenue for the projects we publish on. Our aim at Packt is to establish publishing royalties as an essential part of the service and support a business model that sustains Open Source.

If you're working with an Open Source project that you would like us to publish on, and subsequently pay royalties to, please get in touch with us.

Writing for Packt

We welcome all inquiries from people who are interested in authoring. Book proposals should be sent to author@packtpub.com. If your book idea is still at an early stage and you would like to discuss it first before writing a formal book proposal, contact us; one of our commissioning editors will get in touch with you.

We're not just looking for published authors; if you have strong technical skills but no writing experience, our experienced editors can help you develop a writing career, or simply get some additional reward for your expertise.

About Packt Publishing

Packt, pronounced 'packed', published its first book "Mastering phpMyAdmin for Effective MySQL Management" in April 2004 and subsequently continued to specialize in publishing highly focused books on specific technologies and solutions.

Our books and publications share the experiences of your fellow IT professionals in adapting and customizing today's systems, applications, and frameworks. Our solution-based books give you the knowledge and power to customize the software and technologies you're using to get the job done. Packt books are more specific and less general than the IT books you have seen in the past. Our unique business model allows us to bring you more focused information, giving you more of what you need to know, and less of what you don't.

Packt is a modern, yet unique publishing company, which focuses on producing quality, cutting-edge books for communities of developers, administrators, and newbies alike. For more information, please visit our web site: www.PacktPub.com.

Drupal 6 Themes

ISBN: 978-1-847195-66-1   Paperback: 312 pages

Create new themes for your Drupal 6 site with clean layout and powerful CSS styling

1. Learn to create new Drupal 6 themes

2. No experience of Drupal theming required

3. Techniques and tools for creating and modifying themes

4. A complete guide to the system's themable elements

Learning Drupal 6 Module Development

ISBN: 978-1-847194-44-2   Paperback: 328 pages

A practical tutorial for creating your first Drupal 6 modules with PHP

1. Specifically written for Drupal 6 development

2. Program your own Drupal modules

3. No experience of Drupal development required

4. Know Drupal 5? Learn what's new in Drupal 6

5. Integrate AJAX functionality with the jQuery library

6. Packt donates a percentage of every book sold to the Drupal foundation

Please check **www.PacktPub.com** for information on our titles

4060992

Made in the USA
Lexington, KY
17 December 2009